fat girl,
SKINNY

Amye Archer

ISBN: 978-0-9969887-0-4

The events in this story are true to my memory, but some of the characters are composites of real people who have traveled in and out of my life. Also, all point values are approximate.

Printed in the United States of America

Cover Designed by Patrick McLane
Author Photo by Sami and Penelope Archer

Also by Amye Archer:

A Shotgun Life
Bangs

Big Table Publishing Company
Boston, MA
bigtablepublishing.com

Acknowledgements

When you write a memoir, you are inviting people into your life: the good, the bad, the ugly. So many of my friends and family graciously accepted this invitation, and never faltered in their love and support. I thank you all. Especially:

Stephanie McLane-who read this book as much as I did, who read this book in every incarnation, who lived through most of this story with me, and who has believed in this book from its origin. Thank you for your invaluable feedback, insight, and love. Jenn Kumpas-who has always encouraged me to write about our life together with such honesty. My sister, Jennie, the consummate artist, who constantly reminded me to stay true to the boiling pot of truth in my belly. Thank you to my mother and father for their unyielding support, Samantha and Penelope-for loving their mommy so hard, and my grandmother-who shaped every part of me with her strength and love.

My mentors: Bev Donofrio, who knew when to say "It's not done," even when I didn't want to hear it, and who guided my writing with patience and wisdom. And Becky Bradway, who encouraged me to write a memoir, and saw something in my story when no one else did. Thank you both. This could not be possible without you.

The wonderful agents, editors, friends, and writers who have given me feedback over the years and have rooted for this book to find a home including: Meg Thompson, Sara Pritchard, Gale Martin, Nancy McKinley, and Ellen Finn. And Robin Stratton, who has always believed in me, I hope I made you proud.

The boys who crossed my path during this time, especially Pricey. Thank you for teaching me the bar chords. And Eugene, after all of the pain, we have found the most wonderful friendship. Thank you for believing early, and for always having my back.

Finally, Tim, who built me a home in more ways than one, and who loved me through every revision.

Amye Archer
March, 2016

For Tim

"When you've had enough, you'll know it."
~ Gram

Prologue

The women of Weight Watchers are tough. A gang. The Bloods, the Crips, and the Latin Kings all rolled into one. Sure, we look harmless enough. Ten or fifteen portly women standing like preschoolers in a straight line outside the door, waiting for the loud-mouthed receptionist to swing it open and begin to weigh us. But make no mistake about it. If you cross us, if you come to a meeting already thin and complaining about five extra pounds that you have gained over the winter and need to lose before bikini season, we will cut you. We will grab you with our fat little paws, roll you up into a tiny little ball, and kick your skinny ass out of here. Because this is our turf. The basement of the Northeast Pennsylvania Chapter of the Electrical Workers Union, with its mundane pine paneling and shiny medicinal floors, belongs to us every Thursday night from seven until eight fifteen. So, if you have less than ten pounds to lose, stay home. Get a stomach flu, stick your finger down your throat, or swallow a laxative, we don't care. Just don't come here.

"Ugh, I feel gross," says Sherri (with an i).

"You'll be fine," says a voice from somewhere in the front of the line.

"I had a brownie last night and I swear to God it went right to my ass."

"No, it takes a while to catch up with you. You'll probably see it next week," says a different voice.

"I hate this," sighs Sherri.

I am late, as always, so I am all the way at the tail end of the line and can barely hear the riveting retellings of this week's sins, but I know they are happening. The line snakes around the long thin corridor and is full of women sizing one another up. We smile and greet one another like we are fighters on the same side, sisters in arms, but deep down we are praying for one another's demise. *I am nowhere near as big as she is. Wow, I hope I don't look like that. Who does she think she is, wearing that kind of top?*

There is a certain code of conduct required. You won't find it in your introductory binder or your new "Getting Started" booklet. You have to become one of us to learn it. For instance, you have to get here early. That's one of the unspoken rules. If you're late, you are stuck in a long, very slow moving procession of nerves and anxiety. What you want is a quickie. Hop on the scale, get the good or bad news, leave the money on the counter and move on. The desire to be here first and to avoid the long wait results in a hallway full of overweight women staring at a closed door, clutching their weekly food journals in one hand and thirteen dollars in the other.

It is the middle of December, yet all of us have come dressed as close to naked as we can get without being arrested for indecent exposure. I'm wearing tiny little knit shorts, a tank top, and socks with sandals. You cannot stand barefoot on the scale, another rule. You cannot hear your weight, the specific number, out loud. That is yet another rule. If you do not follow these expectations, you stick out like the new kid in school. We can smell it on you.

When it's my turn, I hand my book and money over to Joan, an elderly woman with shaky hands and a broad smile. My book is my bible. The list of everything that went into my body this week, with the exception of the Snickers Bar (6 pts) and three Tootsie Rolls (2 pts each) I jammed in my mouth only moments earlier in the car. Joan stamps a red PAID over this week's date and motions for me to climb onto the scale.

"Wow, down three more pounds, Amye! Nice work! What's that bring you to now?" she asks loudly, hoping my success will serve as inspiration.

"Um, twenty seven," I answer, barely able to conceal a smile.

"Twenty seven! Wow! Do you hear that everyone? Amye has lost twenty-seven pounds!" Joan announces to the small room where we have all filtered in and taken off our sandals.

The geniuses at Weight Watchers have developed a super-secret system in which everything has a certain points value based on the calories, fiber, and fat that an item contains. These points then consume your life. I have become obsessed with counting points, calories, and grams of fiber. My dinners come in points now. I have become fluent in points. I can look around and see the points in everything. A hamburger made from lean meat and no cheese, five points. The side of broccoli with one pat of butter, two points. A hot dog, no bun, six points. A banana, two points. Baked chicken, two ounces, three points. A delicious, mouth watering Double Whopper with Cheese, twenty-five points. When I am at the supermarket, I see rows and rows of shiny points. I speak in points. I dream of points. I have become a point. If you cut me open I will bleed points.

My best friend, Georgia, who has only a handful of pounds to lose, has agreed to accompany me on this journey. Together, we have developed a language that only we understand.

Me: I am starving, what can I eat for two points?

Her: Can you use Flex?

Me: Maybe, if I go under tomorrow. How about a granola bar?

Her: Too pointy. Can you do a veggie?

Me: Sigh. I guess.

It's a language that draws confused stares from skinny strangers and smiles of recognition from pudgy women in the grocery store.

The shaky receptionist affixes a golden star to my weigh-in booklet, folds everything nice and tight, and sends me on my way.

I wish I could say I had an epiphany that brought me to Weight Watchers. That I had cared so much about my own body, my own health, and my own well being that I dragged my fat ass to the only place I knew could help me. But that was not the case. I'm here because I'm desperate. I'm here because I have nowhere else to go. I'm here because I need help.

As a teenager, I remember reading a book my mother had that was written by Richard Simmons. He described the event that made him lose weight. Apparently, some well meaning Samaritan who loved him but didn't have the guts to criticize him, put a note on his car that said something to the effect of "I love you, please don't die." This changed his life and inspired him to lose weight and begin helping others lose weight. The story fascinated me, not because of the touching moment in which Simmons realized someone cared about him, but because I always thought to myself: *What kind of an asshole would leave a note like that?* I wish I had a Richard Simmons story, but the truth is there was no cute moment like that. I have had plenty of events over the years that should have inspired this change but never did.

I have been in a stuffy elevator and had some guy ask me when my baby was due. I have had the people at work call me an elephant and make cow noises when I walked by. I have stared at myself in a full length mirror, while being wedged by two seamstresses into a size 28 wedding dress. I have been told by a doctor that I will almost certainly contract Type II Diabetes. I have been at an amusement park and left a ride line because I was afraid that the pull down bar would not fit over my stomach. I have been labeled sterile because of my heft. I have had chairs break under my weight in the company of friends. Still, none of these events triggered that moment of inspiration. I wish I could say it happened in one of those ways, because the truth is actually worse. I'm here because of a man.

part one

Chapter One

It was not the *love* of a man that drove me to finally confront my growing waistline; rather, it was the *leaving* of one. Six weeks ago my husband Jack walked out of our two-bedroom apartment. He would not be coming back. Our marriage had actually ended weeks prior, but it wasn't until a Thursday night in November that he actually moved out.

November in my hometown of Scranton, Pennsylvania, could mean rain or snow, depending on the year. That particular night, it was pouring outside. Strings of silver rain pooled and unspooled like thread over the edges of our gutters. I stood silent in the entranceway as Jack loaded his belongings into the car. *Our* car. The new car we couldn't afford but I cosigned for anyway, to keep him happy. The new car he would be taking with him on the journey back to his mother's house.

His shoes squeaked with moisture on the linoleum as he walked past me. We had been at this point before, many times. The shouted ultimatums, the veiled threats, and the promises of abandonment were part of our ongoing dialogue. But this time was different. Jack's eyes were cold and far away. The life we had spent ten years building was imploding, breaking apart from the inside out. In that moment, I felt an emptiness so deep it threatened to drown me. I had to stop him.

"Please don't go," I begged as he shoved his clothes into a giant duffel bag I had been given for opening a bank account with our local credit union.

"Amye," he started, but didn't finish.

"Please, Jack. We can work this out. I know we can." I reached for his shaved head, the gray-stubbed remnants of his once long blonde locks.

"You wanted me gone, you wanted me out. I'm giving you what you wanted." He stared at me. He was waiting for the anger to return. The same anger that often transformed me into a spitting, cursing, and deranged woman. I stayed calm. I had no choice. Any wrong move on my part would cement his leaving forever.

"No, you aren't. You are only leaving because of Sarah. You and I, we always work these things out."

Sarah was his manager at Radio Shack. Sarah was a phone number. Sarah was the voice on the other end of a warm cell phone, the sender of text messages suggesting they meet for a drink. Sarah was a toxin, a poison, the other woman.

I'd discovered her on a gray, mundane morning only two weeks prior. Had woken early, showered, and headed out to the living room to say goodbye before leaving for work. Jack was passed out on the couch after a night of drinking. On the floor next to him sat an empty wine bottle and an overcrowded ash tray. The windows were closed and the smoke was stale and lingering like a fog. His silver cell phone was shoved under the recliner with only a small corner revealing its presence. Its position alarmed me. It looked almost hidden. I flipped open the phone and there it was staring me in the face.

"Jack," I tried to wake him. "Jack!"

He jumped awake and blinked for a few minutes until the room came into focus.

"What?" he asked and smacked his lips together, his mouth dry from sleep.

"What's going on with you and Sarah?" My legs trembled beneath me.

"What do you mean?" He popped up like a spring, then said nothing as I stood there reading the back and forth between him and Sarah out loud, like a performer in some poorly-written play. They ended their messages with Xs and Os. Their tone was familiar. She made reference to buying him an XBOX 360 for Christmas, which retailed for about $500 dollars. I knew the minute I saw that promise that I could never compete. Jack had always been a commodity, easily bought.

All the while, he said nothing in his own defense. There was nothing to say. I was blindsided by his betrayal. If there'd been one constant in my life, it was that Jack needed me. He suffered from debilitating anxiety and was prone to horrible panic attacks. Over our ten plus years together I became the one person who could help him, calm him, bring him back into his body. I was good at it. I knew what to say, how to say it, and how to touch and hold him in a way that reconnected him to the moment. I read books on how to beat his disease, went to every doctor's appointment, and spent countless hours studying ways to cure him of the anxiety inside of him. Even when he didn't want to put forth the same effort. I never thought he would leave me. I counted on him needing me.

Over the next two weeks, Jack flip-flopped in his convictions. He disappeared for days at a time, shacking up at Sarah's house, while I sat home crying and wondering what his next move would be. Then, when Sarah inevitably pushed him from his comfort zone, or his conscience got the best of him, his mind would change and the ground between us would weaken, sending me land-sliding back into his arms.

I obsessed over Sarah. How could she allow such behavior? *How could I?* I had met her a handful of times at the store where they worked. She greeted me by name, told me how lucky she was to have Jack as an employee, demonstrated lovely manners, and never let on they were romantically involved. The obsession was consuming me. A choice had to be made. In the end, Jack chose Sarah.

The rain outside continued to pound the roof of our bedroom. Jack said nothing as he finished packing. I rubbed his back and shoulders, reminding him of my touch. His black T-shirt was damp from the rain and stuck to his back. He was thick and fifty pounds overweight, unlike when we first met, when he was seventeen and so skinny I was often afraid he would slip through my fingers.

"Amye, come on. Stop it." When he pushed me from him, I collapsed backwards on the bed, my stomach like a lake, sending ripples of fat up the front of my body, crashing against my chin.

"I can't believe you're doing this," I sobbed. Tears mixed with snot and streamed down my face in clear, sticky ribbons. "I will do anything, please."

"Amye–" Jack looked up at me from his boxes. "We agreed to this." For the first time, he was the rational one. *He* was the one who wanted out, not me.

"We've agreed to this 900 times in the past, but we always work it out." I felt like a teenager who wished her mother dead, only to have it happen. I felt like I was on an operating table and they were pulling organs from my chest cavity one at a time. I replayed the many times I had thrown in the towel on our relationship. The words I screamed, the hatred I felt, the betrayal, the neglect, they spun around in my memory like a carousel, just memories melting into one another. That night it was like a light went out between us. I had become invisible. He was right. I had said those words. I was unhappy, but I wasn't ready to be without that unhappiness yet.

As Jack stood up to leave, I sprang from the bed and threw my arms around his thick neck. "Please don't do this, I don't want this. I've changed my mind. I want a reset. Please, I am scared," I whispered into his moist skin.

"I have to go." He pulled my arms from around him like he

was shrugging off a an old coat, and walked out the front door.

I thought about chasing after him, begging, pleading, or promising anything I could think of: pizza every night, new video games weekly, a blow job every evening after dinner. Whatever would get him to stay. But something was holding me back. Something pressed my lips tightly together, tied my hands together behind my back, and prevented me from moving. A small whisper of a voice calling out from the center of me. *Let him go.*

Chapter Two

I met Jack at a local pool hall when I was sixteen. He wore red Chuck Taylors, and when we spoke he recited poetry and discussed literature with such ease that I fell in love with him immediately. He was the smartest and most well-read person I had ever met. He was two years older than me, and light years ahead of guys my own age.

I have a picture of us taken only days after we met. We are standing in a friend's living room. I'm not yet fat, just a little chunky, and my black hair hangs silky and straight to the middle of my back. Jack is wearing a Nirvana shirt and a jean jacket, and his pencil thin arm is draped around me. He's not looking at the camera. He's staring at me. And that's how it was most of the time. I was his world.

Then, before we knew what hit us, Jack was sick. Jack needed care. I took care of Jack. Jack needed me. This quickly became our relationship. It was a pattern of codependency that lasted the entire ten years of our relationship. I resented his disease. I resented him. Yet I loved him and stayed with him because he needed me. It was the right thing to do.

And now, it was over. Without Jack needing me, I don't know who I am anymore. I feel like I have just had my legs removed, and I can't quite figure out how to walk. I know our relationship was toxic. A term learned from my mother's subtle gift-giving. She had purchased enough self help books for me over the years that I eventually sat down and read one. I understand that Jack and I were both trapped together out of fear: fear of the unknown, fear of being alone, fear of losing one another. I know that we brought out the worst in each another. But the logical mind has nothing on that gaping hole inside of my gut and I am spiraling downward into a black hole. I need a life raft, something I can control. Then, one day in the break room at work, I overhear two women talking about Weight Watchers, and soon I am drawn like a magnet to the bright florescent lights of the International Brotherhood of Electrical Workers building.

Signing up for Weight Watchers is a lot like being shoved into a Kindergarten classroom for the first time. There's a way to do things. You must be acclimated to the routine. First, there's the paperwork. You are seated at a small folding table at the back of the room and asked to fill out the following: name, address, the "please don't sue us if this doesn't work or works too well" waiver, and finally in a small box, there is room for your weight loss goal. My mind searches for the right answer, for my goal. I consider writing: skinny, not disgusting, anything but what I am now, not heartbroken, or simply normal. But the box seems to beg for a number. I write 165. A hundred pounds lighter than I am at this moment.

"This goal is not right," the shaky receptionist, Joan, says in a whisper after I hand her my materials. "How tall are you?"

"Five two."

"Your ideal range is between 120 and 135."

135? Is this woman crazy? 135? It seems almost impossible, like it's a number attainable only by space shuttle. A number that lives in Atlantis, that's carried around on the back of the Lochness, a number I will *never* see.

"Well, I think I'll stick to 165. That's a hundred pounds," I point out, just in case she's as bad at math as I am.

There are whispers between her and the tall woman sitting next to her. Then, a reluctant smile. "Okay dear."

After all of that, the woman opens a book and begins to explain the program. There are two aspects to the Weight Watcher's plan. One is the plan itself. You are supplied with the proper materials, you make the right decisions, and you return every week to be weighed. Then, there's the network of support. In a room adjoining the weigh station, there are meetings held that are akin to a support group for people like me, struggling to lose weight. *It's all very simple*, the woman assures me, *you'll do great*. Finally, I am ushered into the meeting room, where I will be under the care of a group leader, someone who will change my life. Someone who will show me the way: former fatty and community-college dropout, Pam.

Pam is in her late fifties with a killer body and a bouncing bob that gathers neatly at her pronounced jaw line. She wears a different pastel-colored pantsuit each week, earning her the nickname Pantsuit Pam. She is someone who has already lost weight and can motivate us to do the same. She is Scranton's own version of Richard Simmons. I wonder to myself if anyone has ever left a note on *her* car.

The group sessions are useless to me at first. A lot of introductory bullshit. There are always eight or ten of us, at least, but some weeks there are more. As a new member, you are asked to stand up and introduce yourself. There's a lot of squeaking and pleading from the metal chairs during this time. When it is my turn, I cut it short. *I'm Amye. I'm twenty-six. My starting weight was two hundred and sixty-five pounds. I eat too much.* I don't have the heart to tell them that I am getting divorced, that I filed the papers two days after my husband left, and that he is currently sleeping with a blonde Republican. It's all too embarrassing.

It goes on like this for weeks. Then, one night, a few weeks before the Christmas holiday, the meetings become important. I hear a phrase that will forever change how I remember my weight gain, how I view my history, and how I handle my weight-loss journey. That phrase is "food addiction." *Foooddd Addicction.* Pam says the phrase with too many syllables and too many vowels. But when those words leave her mango orange lips, it's as if a dead soldier inside of me suddenly stands up.

I never knew where my fat came from. It was a mystery that has haunted my entire family. I was as skinny as a rail until I was about twelve. My mother still talks about how I wore slim fit jeans for *as long as she can remember*. I was shaped like a match stick, flat-chested and long, with a head attached. Then I hit puberty, and then came curves, lots of them. My breasts began to grow at an alarming rate, making me the most popular girl in school, even though my stomach was beginning to swell and my neck was becoming thick, jiggling like pancake batter.

To my parents, this was the worst fate I could have bestowed on them. A fat daughter. Sure they still loved me, but they were raging pragmatists and in their eyes my weight loss was a problem they could not solve. My father dragged me to the gym with him every night. He ran the indoor track that circled the basketball courts, while I walked for miles on a treadmill on the balcony overhead. After almost a year's time, when he noticed the scale was still climbing the other way—the numbers running further away from us—he gave up trying.

My mother took more of a nutritional approach. She began "closing" the kitchen at seven o'clock, fending off any ideas I had of night time snacking. She stocked the refrigerator with only the bare essentials needed to survive: yogurt, ketchup, and an occasional bunch of grapes. She slipped veggies into my lunch pail, refused to order pizza, and never carried a bag of chips over the threshold.

But what my family didn't know, what none of us knew, was that I was in the throes of an addiction. That even though I was fourteen, fifteen, sixteen years old, and subject to living under their roof, I was still allowed a certain amount of freedom. With that freedom, I stuffed candy bars into my purse at the store after school, bartered for cupcakes with my friends at lunchtime, and ate fast food every single chance I got. I worked at McDonalds, so having access to chicken nuggets and strawberry milkshakes every weekend was guaranteed.

By the time I reached college, my parents were starting to panic. My father had gone from encouraging me to exercise, to bribery. *Lose fifty pounds and we will buy you a whole new wardrobe*, he told me one night while I was living in State College. It was becoming a crisis. Next to my older sister, Jennie, and her size-one figure, I looked like a grizzly bear ready to swallow my own offspring. My father is a mathematician at heart and in his mind this should have been so easy: less calories + more exercise = less weight (less chins) + more self esteem (less Jack). Only, he had no idea what he was up against. My father and my mother were powerless against the gaping hole inside of me.

By the time I was twenty, I was binging almost nightly on fast food. I was eating two or three cheeseburgers, fries, milkshakes, whatever I could fit. And when I felt my stomach ballooning from being full, I simply took a deep breath and waited for a few minutes before shoving more food down my throat. My parents never knew about my addiction because I never let them. I had a set of lies I lived by:

1. The lies I told others:

I couldn't bring my food home and I could never eat inside of the restaurant. No one could see me because then I would be discovered. Eating was a private indulgence and it had to remain hidden from the world. "I don't eat fast food," I would say. I was the picture of health aside from my expanding waistline and multiplying chins.

2. The lies I told myself:

This will be my last time. I will stop eating fast food starting tomorrow. I had a really bad day at work. I deserve this, I have a terribly boring life. I'm pressed for time, it's easier to grab fast food.

23

And then there was Jack. So forgiving and so in love with me that he not only accepted this behavior, but he participated in the festivities. When we lived together, I was sent out for Burger King, McDonalds, Wendy's, or Arby's, three nights a week at least. I would return home carrying a fifteen pound bag containing four sandwiches, two large fries, and two very large sodas with their weight distributed evenly in a cardboard cup holder. Together, we were like two lions feasting on a buffet of gazelles.

Of course this was food addiction. *Of course*. That explains everything. But wasn't the compulsion to eat a problem for every fat person? Aren't we all food addicts in some form? The only other alternative is that we are stupid and don't understand nutrition. It's a lack of self-control. It's an inherent laziness. That's what skinny people think. They think we are stupid, out of control, lazy people. But the truth is, we are sick and sad, and we need Pantsuit Pam to guide us through this disease, to make us well.

Chapter Three

Thanksgiving is a complete disaster. I spend the whole morning staring a hole through my cell phone. I am convinced Jack will call, and when my phone remains cold and silent, I can't hold back the tears. This is our first Thanksgiving apart, our first holiday away from one another. I work on busying my mind with other things. I scrub the kitchen floor, clean the toilets, wash the bathtub out, and figure out my point allowance for the day. I plan to eat three ounces of turkey, a cup of stuffing, and two ounces of cranberry sauce for a total of 11 points give or take (I'm being generous on the cranberry sauce). I try not to care that I will not be sitting on the plastic lawn chairs pulled into Jack's mother's kitchen, eating turkey doused with gravy from a jar, and the chocolate cheesecake that is always sure to follow.

My heartbreak is bipolar. Most days I miss Jack like I missed living with my college roommate after she moved out. It's strange not having someone else in the house with me. I miss the safety in knowing that no matter what the outside world would throw at me, I had someone at home that needed me and wasn't going anywhere, far. I miss the floor creaking near the bathroom late at night, the smell of his aftershave in the still steamy bathroom after a shower, and the sound of the gravel in the driveway kicking up as he arrived home from work. The pain is there, but it's relegated to heartache, not heartbreak. Sometimes at night, I can actually feel the weight off my shoulders since he left, and I become almost giddy with the possibilities spread out before me as a single person.

Then there's days like today, when I miss Jack so much I feel like my heart will explode and splatter my guts all over the light blue walls of our empty house. Today is one of those bad days. It is my first hurdle to overcome, my first real test of strength. There will be more, but the first is the most important.

For Thanksgiving Dinner, I agree to accompany my sister, Jennie, and her boyfriend to dinner at a friend's house. Going anywhere at all is against my better judgment, but Jennie thinks it will be good for me. I resist and refuse, but she convinces me that it might help take my mind off the dissolution of my entire life that happened only days prior. I put down the toilet brush, throw on jeans and a t-shirt, and ride in the backseat like a prisoner.

I regret my decision only minutes after we arrive. These strangers are friends of Jennie's boyfriend. I barely know them, yet we all know them so well: the two perfectly talented and cheery blonde children who come home from college every chance they get because "no one can beat Mom's cooking!", the attractive father who goes often (willingly) to the ballet with his wife and actually cares about who his kids are dating and what they are studying in school, and finally, the beautiful mother, around whom they all swirl. She is elegant and sophisticated, with the top button always fastened on her cardigan. Today she is limiting herself to only one glass of wine an hour. "Gotta watch my figure," she announces as she runs her hands down her size three hips.

Where the fuck am I? I feel like I'm watching a bad romantic comedy, and I'm the spinster sidekick that will never have this life. I want to gag. I want to puke chunks of their perfectly cooked turkey all over their reupholstered furniture. I want to take my oversized glass of wine with the name I can't pronounce and smash it right over their fucking heads.

Instead, I float like an excommunicated sinner along the outside walls watching the scene in front of me as it becomes a living, breathing Norman Rockwell painting. Finally, when the golden-haired daughter takes to the baby grand piano, I lose it. A yelp escapes my lips as tears begin streaming down my face. The picture in front of me becomes a still-life. Everyone turns and stares.

"I'm sorry," I manage to mutter through my blubbering lips.

I slam my wine glass down on the sofa table without using a coaster, dash through the living room and out the back door where I flop down onto the cold stone stoop overlooking a perfectly manicured yard. My head falls into my hands as I weep. *Here we go again.* The crying has become a problem. Like a covert operator it sneaks its way into everyday situations: work, conversations with friends, the drive home, the laundry room, and then when you least expect it, it explodes, revealing itself. I cry in front of random strangers, bartenders, friends, relatives, store clerks, and the mailman. Any little thing sets me off. A touching moment on TV, a song on the radio, someone asking if I'm okay, the tone in a mother's voice, the mere presence of my father, or the smell of Newport cigarettes. And no one knows what to do about it when it happens, including me. Last week I actually locked my office door and crammed my fat body under my desk where I shook with sobs for a good hour before climbing back out.

On the porch, behind me, a screen door slaps against its wooden frame.

"You need to pull it together, Aim," Jennie says as she sits down next to me. She rubs her bare arms with her hands for warmth.

"I can't help it, Jennie," I say.

"You're acting like a crazy person."

"I'm not crazy, Jennie. I'm fucking devastated, can't you see that?" My voice is hoarse and I have to push everything out.

In a rare moment of tenderness, my sister runs her long, thin fingers up and down my back. "It's hard around the holidays," she says, "but it will get better. I promise."

Suddenly I am so grateful for her, her soft voice, her bony shoulder under my head. Four years older than me, her desire to protect me is a reflex, an echo from our shared past. She knows me better than anyone, knows my potential, and believes I can be something. Jennie knows that once I am past this bleakness, there will be light. She's convinced of it.

The two of us sit on the back porch for a while as I collect myself. The perfect family hosts the perfect party in the windows behind us. Muffled laughter and my occasional sniffle are the only sounds. The air is thin and cold. In the yard before us the red, green, yellow, and orange leaves are scattered like dead soldiers on a battlefield, stretched out against the fading green canvas.

Chapter Four

With the agony of Thanksgiving behind me, I have moved into the next phase of my grieving: anger. As I replay the events of the last few weeks in my head over and over again: the text messages between Jack and Sarah, the distance in Jack's eyes, his lack of concern for my heartbreak, and the fact that he hasn't called me once, *not once*, to see how I'm faring. I am pissed off. Angrier than I have ever been in my life. Unlike heartbreak that comes and goes, anger seems to have set up camp inside of me. There are no days without anger, there are just days with *less* anger.

Some days I want to drive to Sarah's house with a gallon of

lighter fluid and torch everything inside. Then, some days, I simply add her phone number to a telemarketing list, or sign them both up for junk mail. But it's not enough. I want them to suffer for what they did to me. I want to see them writhe in pain and regret. I want to see their lives ripped out from under them like mine was. I assure myself that I will inevitably see one or both of them again. It's only a matter of time. And that's one meeting I *will* be ready for. I will strategize and prepare myself. I'm going Machiavelli on their asses. I have told no one of my plans. Until tonight.

Pantsuit Pam wants us to examine the impetus, the reason for our fat bottoms being in these seats. Dottie, an older woman with a curler still in the back of her hair (I cannot deduce if it's intentional or not) shoots her arm through the air.

"I want to fit into a bikini this summer," she says with excitement brimming in her eyes. She goes on and on about a yellow bathing suit she wore in her twenties, *maaaany years ago*, she adds (and we agree). She is determined to wear the suit again next summer. Dottie is an instant enigma. She is dressed to the nines, black pants that look as if the pleat has been intentionally ironed in, a floral blouse, perfectly curled ash-brown hair, and a silver bracelet dangling from her wrist. But then, there's that curler. That pink spongy oddity. The one detail she has forgotten. Like a CSI, I begin drawing conclusions about Dottie. She must live alone, or with someone who hates her. Otherwise she would have been told about the barnacle. Unhappy marriage perhaps? She must drive with perfect posture, not allowing her head to hit the headrest and discover the bump against her brain. Maybe she was a ballerina? Perfect posture is practically one of the requirements. I chuckle at the thought of Dottie on toe shoes.

"Excuse me, would you like to share?" Pantsuit Pam's gaze is fixed on me.

"Oh, I, um," I mutter.

"What is your reason for losing weight?" she repeats the question that is written in pretty pink chalk behind her. The crowd turns to look at me. Dottie, the unhappily married ballerina, frowns as she sits in her seat prematurely.

I run through the possible answers in my head: If I don't lose this weight I will never find a replacement for Jack. I will die an old fat lady in my bed, and the city will have to crane me out of there like the mother in *What's Eating Gilbert Grape*. The fear of public humiliation. It's a constant in a fat person's life.

Pantsuit Pam and the others are growing impatient. I search my brain for the appropriate lie. I could say I'm concerned about my health, that I want to one day run a marathon, or that I am trying to avoid the inevitable diabetes that I'm sure is coming my way. I could say any of those things and a smile would sprout on Pantsuit Pam's perfectly plump lips, but I don't. I can't lie to her. She is like the Medusa of dishonesty. If you tell her a lie you will turn to stone.

"Revenge," I say, not rising from my chair. The room falls deadly silent. Some women fix their gaze on me, but most turn to Pam for her reaction.

"Excuse me?"

"I'm here out of revenge."

Pantsuit Pam's fingers lock together behind her head. Her elbows are pointy and pink. She is a coach whose team has just lost the big game. A deep and heavy breath escapes her lips and her hair bounces against her forehead.

"Okay," she says with a resigned tone, "Let's hear this one."

"My husband left me. He's dating the woman he left me for. I want to lose a shitload of weight so that when I see him again he wants me back. It's pretty simple really."

"So you want him back?" Pantsuit Pam leans forward in her chair, suddenly intrigued.

"Nope. I just want him to think that. That way he'll break up with her, come back to me, and I can reject him." It made sense last night in my empty apartment after four glasses of wine. Now, it sounds like something a thirteen year old thought up.

29

For the first time in the weeks I have been here, Pantsuit Pam is speechless. Dottie stares at me with pity. The others mumble and laugh. My answer catapults Pam into a twenty minute dissertation on the health risks of being overweight. She stresses the fact that your journey to thin has to come from a desire for a better life. If you are losing weight for anyone else, you will not stick to it. You will inevitably fail, because the pure intention is not there. *She obviously has never been dumped*, I think to myself. This plan of mine is giving me something to do, something to focus on, a reason to get out of bed in the morning. It's all I have.

It doesn't occur to me that I am setting myself up for failure or that I have begun this change in my life under all the wrong pretenses. I'm hurt and confused and I can't eat. The weight simply drops off like an anchor falling to the ocean floor.

Chapter Five

"You know what you need?"

"What?" I ask.

"To sleep with someone else. Pronto."

My best friend, Georgia, has a better idea. After spending over an hour on the phone with me listening to my pathetic revenge fantasy, she's decided to take action. She's decided that it's *about goddamn time you find someone else*. And while my sister's advice involves getting to know the inner me, creating a map of my future, and finding solace in being single, there is a growing desperation inside of me that she cannot understand, a starving animal that is beginning to chew its way out. And it is for this reason that Georgia's idea wins out.

In Scranton, people usually meet each other in one of two places: a church or a bar. The reason being is that there is practically one of each on every street corner. Since I am not a religious person, I start with the latter. The New Nickel is one of these corner bars. The exterior is a boring brown brick illuminated only with a blinking neon Coors Light logo, of which the "ight" has burned out.

"I can't do this, Georgia. I feel weird," I say over the static hum of the neon. It's a Friday night in December, and Georgia and I find ourselves standing outside The New Nickel staring at the plain facade.

"Shut up. You can do this. You look fantastic," she reminds me. "Twenty-seven pounds, Aim."

Georgia shrugs off my last minute panic and shoves me through the black battered door. The first thing we see is a long U-shaped bar wrapping itself around the room like a horseshoe with old men perfectly plotted twelve to eighteen inches apart drinking from small clear glasses. A young bartender with a shaved head and pink skin is ping ponging between them. He looks Georgia up and down as we approach. He sees what they all see, that she is beautiful and confident. I am invisible next to her.

We grab two beers and make our way to the back of the room. I have to hold my breath through the cloud of smoke as we walk. At the very rear of the room against a fully carpeted wall, a local band is setting up their equipment. The guitar player plugs a spider web of electrical cords into a single outlet. The lights dim every time he turns on his amp, and a low buzz can be heard over the three speakers mounted against the yellow drop ceiling that runs the length of the room.

"Do you suppose this is a fire hazard?" I ask Georgia as we watch with Miller Lite bottles sweating in our hands.

"Will you relax?" She glares at me.

I trust Georgia. I trust that she would never sleep with my boyfriend (should I ever have one again). I trust that she will never steal from me. I trust that she will never embarrass me on a reality show for her own gain. I trust that she would help me bury a body, escape from prison, or rob a bank. But I do not trust her romantic advice, not when I'm in my right mind anyway. I have been friends with Georgia since we were five years old, and if there's one thing I

31

know, it's that we have very different ideas on love. Her parents' marriage was tenuous at best, having stretched and strained over three children and two different sets of alcohol problems. There were years when her parents didn't even speak to each other, when divorce loomed over Georgia's home like a dark cloud brimming with rain. When they finally did speak, it was often in violence and anger, insults floating between thrown knickknacks and broken dishes.

While I've always considered myself to be a diehard romantic who needs to be wooed and wowed into and out of bed, Georgia's romantic view is closer to that of her home life: all action and not much talking. She is the closest thing to a guy in a girl's body that I have ever seen. She has been married since the age of twenty, but the three or four sexually active years before she met her current husband were filled with one night stands and not much regret. She is the type of woman who sets her sights on a man, sleeps with him, and moves on. A quality I've always secretly envied her for.

Now, I was reaping the benefits of her detachment. She had become the master, and I the apprentice. She plotted our next move, this move, this night. The New Nickel was picked not for its gaudy decor and ancient inhabitants, but because of its proximity to my ex-boyfriend's house. An ex that Georgia believes will serve as the perfect rebound from the breakup of my marriage. Twenty minutes into the band's opening set, her gamble pays off.

"There he is," she yells into my ear and motions with her head to the opposite side of the bar.

"Oh my God." My stomach flips. There, across the bar was my ex-boyfriend, Ryan, just as Georgia had predicted. Ryan and I dated for a year when I was only fifteen, almost sixteen. He taught me everything I know about sex. He schooled me in the ways of teenage humping with the city as our classroom: in pricker bushes behind the old baseball field, on the banks of the Lackawanna river, and behind the firehouse in North Scranton, just to name a few.

Before Georgia and I can adequately discuss how much older

Ryan looks, how much weight he's put on, or how much hair he's lost, he spots us and makes his way over. I jab Georgia in the rib cage with my left elbow. My palms start to sweat.

"Hey there!" he exclaims as he reaches us.

"Hey Ryan!" Georgia proclaims like she hasn't been staring at him for the last ten minutes.

"Hi Amye, how are you?"

"I'm good, Ryan, how about yourself?"

In the next five minutes Georgia becomes nonexistent. She is merely wallpaper, a prop and a backdrop, as Ryan and I reestablish the sexual chemistry once palpable between us so many years ago. We inch closer as the music grows louder. Finally, Ryan pulls me by the arm to a side table, away from the black, pumping speakers. His touch sends a familiar heat through my body.

"So how the hell are you? You look fantastic by the way," he yells.

"Thanks!" And then it hits me. A feeling of shame and embarrassment. I remember seeing him a few years ago at a local grocery store. I was married and fat, and zigzagged my way around the produce department to avoid him. He caught up with me around the bananas. I'm immediately brought back to that place, that feeling of insecurity, that knee jerk reaction to avoid familiar faces for fear of their pitiful looks and hurtful comments whispered behind my back.

"Well it was good catching up," I announce and start pulling away as the band stops playing, the lights brighten, and the newly installed jukebox springs to life with a slow Elvis tune.

"Wait, wait just a minute!" Ryan says and with one hand around my waist he pulls me into him. "Where do you think you're going? I thought we were catching up," he slurs into my neck.

His breath warms my neck as his hands find their way to the very tip of my jean's back pocket. His calloused skin rubs the thick denim covering my ass. I love these jeans. I love the way I feel in these jeans. My skinny (er) jeans. My size sixteen, the-very-first-pairof-jeans-I-ever-bought-in-a-normal-sized-store jeans. My I-don't-care-if-it-takes-two-hours-and-a-can-of-Crisco-I'm-wearing-them-tonight jeans. I don't know if it's the four Miller Lites, Ryan's hands on my body, or the smell of his cologne, but suddenly I am familiar with him and the years we spent apart snap away like a stretched-out rubber band suddenly released. I'm swaying my hips toward him as we talk and seductively reapplying my lip-gloss every chance I get. He laughs at everything I say and leans in close to better hear me.

Minutes later in the bathroom, with the music of the band's second set pumping loudly through the walls, Georgia and I reconvene.

"Oh my God, oh my God," I keep repeating. My heart is racing.

"Get a hold of yourself," Georgia orders with her hands on my shoulders.

"He's still pretty hot, don't you think?" I break away from her and head into one of the stalls.

"No," she answers through her funneled mouth as she reapplies her ruby-red lipstick.

"Aw, come on Georgia, he's still…Ryan."

"Eh, you know how I feel. He's all yours." She drags out the word "all" like a ribbon.

"Georgia!" I yell over the flush of the toilet. It's unusually dark in the bathroom which makes me question why my black heels keep sticking to the floor.

"I can't help it," she says, "I never thought he was hot."

"So, what's the plan?" I ask.

"Okay, so in like a half an hour, I'll get a phone call and say I have to leave."

The ride home. Classic. Not that I have ever been in a bar as a single woman before. Everything I've learned about this lifestyle I've learned from television sitcoms or soap operas.

The bathroom door at The New Nickel doesn't touch the

floor. It is a cheap half door probably borrowed from a bathroom stall and hung on the hinges of the main doorway. It's unnerving to think the entire club can see your feet as you pace back and forth on the dirty floor deciding your fate. It's a puppet show with shoes.

Twenty minutes later, the band has reappeared and is well into a mediocre rendition of Stone Temple Pilot's "Plush" when Georgia makes her exit. Ryan and I are swaying to the music, smiling at one another, and working on our six or seventh beer when she drops the news. Ryan announces that he would be *more than happy* to get me home safely. Within seconds, Georgia is gone and my life is in Ryan's hands. He moves in closer and I can smell the scent of too many Marlboros on him. The band slows, and a slightly off-pitch version of an Aerosmith ballad pours from the speakers. As we rock together, I become that young girl he once found devastatingly beautiful again. I am pre-Jack. My skin is tight, my face is smooth, my body is thin and soft. I am sexy.

Ryan's lips are rough and hard, scraping my skin as he explores my upper body. We are in the parking lot behind The New Nickel in Ryan's rusted out work van. It has been ten years since I tasted another man's kiss. Now, tangling tongues with Ryan in the middle of the dark night, I know I can take this as far as I want with no consequences. There is no one home waiting for me. No one to tell me to stop. No ring on my finger to ruin my fun. It is both exhilarating and terrifying. I am operating on a cocktail of nervous energy and adrenaline.

As Ryan's hands slide across my naked belly, I panic and realize that I don't know the rules of this game anymore. I am ignorant to the intricacies of the single person's sexual code. I don't know how far you can go forward before pulling back. I don't know if pulling back is even an option. Ryan doesn't seem to sense my hesitation and slides on top of me. My bare back sticks to the cold leather seats. His tongue navigates between my breasts. This is it. I am going to do this. I am going to have unmarried sex.

"Wait, Ryan," I peel us apart.

"What?"

"Let's go to my place. I don't want to do this in a car."

Ryan drives me home like a blind man, swerving onto the shoulder and vibrating over the rumble strips as he rubs my inner thigh from the driver seat. We pull into my driveway and I am jarred back into heartbreak. My car sits there, alone, with no partner. It's awkward, like seeing an adult missing a front tooth. I wonder for a split second where Jack is at this very moment.

Ryan slides from the driver seat and the whole van shakes as he slams his door. He walks around the rear of the van and I watch him in the mirror with his back to me as he waters my lawn with his piss. Left alone, my nerves start to take over. With Jack there was a language, an unspoken foreplay, to which I grew accustomed. I haven't slept with Ryan, or anyone else for that matter, since I was sixteen years old. I don't speak his language anymore. Do I have to undress fully, or was it acceptable to leave my panties bound around my ankles as I had with Jack? I have no condoms in the house, therefore no way of preventing an STD. And my legs. Sure, I shaved them before I left, but not above the knee. Should I have shaved above the knee? Will he even be exploring up that high? What about a blowjob? Are they required now? How will he communicate to me that a blowjob is desired? Am I supposed to just know?

The heat in Ryan's van is broken and I can see my breath freeze and fall as it hits the window while I wait for him to appear. Suddenly, he swings my door open, the rusty hinges squeaking in the dead silence of one o'clock in the morning, and reaches up for my hand. I place my right heel on the step side and begin my descent from Ryan's chariot that, according to the faded logo on the side, once belonged to Roto Rooter. Suddenly, before he can catch me, I fall face down in my front yard, onto a frozen pile of dead grass and slush. My jeans absorb the thawing juices. I lay there for a second trying to decide if I can recover with any sex appeal still intact.

"Oh my God, are you okay?" Ryan chuckles over me. His voice blankets the air around us. I look to make sure my neighbors haven't heard our arrival. I glance across the street at my sister Jennie's apartment building. The windows are still dark. What would my neighbors think? My husband only gone a few weeks.

"Yes," I say, rising to my knees and rubbing my elbows in pain. I'm soaked.

We are not even in the door for thirty seconds before he has me pinned against a pine-paneled wall in my hallway, kissing my neck and my face. It feels good. I feel good. I am down almost thirty pounds now, and for the first time I can remember, I am actually inviting a man to touch my body. Next to us a propane wall heater whistles faintly, one large orange brick glowing with fire illuminates our faces. Ryan was always a fantastic kisser, and still is. He moves his hands up to my face, cradles my newly protruding jaw line, and pushes his tongue deep inside my mouth. His other hand, at the nape of my neck, tugs my hair slightly, sending a surge of electricity through my body. We are like shadows the two of us, wrapped together in the pitch dark.

"Swurs vur vedvum?" he whispers with his tongue still deep inside my mouth.

"What?"

"Swurs vur vedvum?" he repeats.

"What?"

He pulls his tongue from my mouth and looks at me. "Where is your bedroom?" he over annunciates.

I freeze. *I am not ready for this. I will fuck this up, guaranteed. I am still too fat. I will do something wrong or lame and he will tell every single man in Scranton that I am a bad lay. I am still too fat. He will see the flabby skin under these jeans and go running for the hills. I am still too fat.* The door to Jack's computer room is only five feet away from us. I can still hear the ghost of him bursting from the room to refill his wine glass or light a new smoke.

"Ryan, I can't do this," I whisper. "I want to stop. Okay?"

"Okay," he mumbles with a mouthful of my right breast.

I struggle to get my shirt back on, but he pushes it further down my arms.

"Really, Ryan, I'm serious." I say and push his chest away from mine, "I'm not ready to do this."

"Fuck!" He stands up straight and runs his hands through his thinning hair. "Fuck!"

"I'm sorry," I say.

"Okay, okay. I understand. That's fine."

"I'm sorry, really I am."

"No, it's fine. I get it." He looks for the doorknob in the dark hallway. I'm afraid to turn on the light, afraid for him to get a good look at what just happened. I just want him to leave, but to come back and do this again tomorrow, and the next day, and the day after that.

"I'll call you," he says and gives me a quick kiss on the forehead.

I want to grab onto him and say, *"Do you promise? Promise me you will really call, cross your heart, and swear an oath. Come back and sleep with me so I can forget Jack, forget the hollow space inside of me, and move on with my life?"* But all I can muster is, "thanks." And the door slams behind him. I slide my shirt back over my shoulders as I try to digest the night's events. I watch through the window as Ryan's van pulls away from view. The apartment is dark except for a nightlight in the kitchen that works on a sensor. *At least one good thing has come from this*, I think to myself, *I'm drunk enough to pass out.*

Chapter Six

Ryan's efficiency apartment hangs off the side of a perfectly manicured duplex like an abscess. As I navigate the maze of dried brown hedge and partially lifted sidewalks, the cold winter air whips around me and practically pushes me to his wooden door. The paint peels under my palms as I feel for a doorbell or knocker in the darkness. The main house is beautifully lit with sconces and little solar pegs illuminating its front sidewalk. The owners have tastefully decorated for Christmas, white candles in the windows and a glowing wreath hanging from a peg on the front door. The only light on Ryan's side of the house is a series of flashes coming from what I presume is the television inside.

It's a crisp, cold Saturday night and barring any unforeseen disasters, it will be *the* night. The night I finally have sex with someone other than Jack. The preparation has been intense. After last weekend's letdown, I was afraid he would never call me again. Then, this morning at around ten, my phone shook with Ryan's ringtone. I tried to disguise the surprise in my voice. He said he thought it was cute that I sent him packing last weekend and that he wanted to make sure I was ready before we had sex. I thought it was cute that he confused sheer terror with self-respect. We made plans for tonight. I mentioned that I would cook him dinner, he replied that he had a very limited kitchen and that food would not be necessary.

Ryan is a textbook example of a boy whose best days were in high school. His looks, while better than most, are not extraordinary. His hair and eyes are a plain brown. His height is average as is his stature. I imagine you could use the same two crayons to complete his portrait: brown and tan. So, while you may not be that impressed at first, it's his smile that gets you. The rarely seen, yet widely coveted parting of his lips to reveal a grin so wide and warm, it makes me want to roll up into a ball and live in the dimples it creates, even now after all this time. I fell for Ryan when I was fifteen and in one night, after one smile in the middle of a dive bar almost twelve years later, here I am falling again.

When he opens the door tonight, however, the smile is absent. He is visibly inconvenienced by my arrival twenty minutes early and has yet to straighten up. I look around and wonder how much time cleaning this place would entail. His apartment consists of only two rooms: a kitchen with mismatched appliances and open shelves rather than cabinets and a living room with a couch smothered with a stained sleeping bag. I follow him to the living room where a small television is playing Seinfeld.

"Oh, I love this one," I say and sit down on the thick blanketed couch. I sit carefully to control my muffin top from popping out above the rim of my jeans. I place my purse on a small wooden table next to the couch, afraid to set it on the discolored carpet. Ryan sits next to me on the couch, but far enough away that you can drive a Volkswagen between us.

"Oh yeah?"

"Yeah, it's the one where George moves back in with his parents and Elaine breaks up with the guy over his punctuation," I tell him.

"Oh. Yeah, that's a good one," Ryan answers.

I hate this. The agony of small talk. I want to fast forward through this part: *how are you? How is the weather? Do you like your job? What's your blood type? Did you feel loved by your parents?* I want to grab the remote and skip to the part that should have happened last weekend if only I hadn't chickened out. I want Ryan to shut off the television and rip my clothes off. I want him to ravish me like Fabio ravishes those women on the covers of cheap romance novels at the supermarket cash register.

I honestly imagine it happening that way. Probably because I had slept with only a handful of boys in my adolescence, and it had been a long ten years since I initiated sex with anyone but my husband. Ten years since my last "first time," Jack and I in my father's pickup truck down by the river on a cool night in March. It was the same night I learned about Jack's disease, a disease that would eventually end up tethering me to him for many years to come.

We were parked by the Lackawanna River, a river in Northeast Pennsylvania heavily contaminated from decades of strip mining. I was on the passenger seat, reclined, and wearing just my underwear and bra. Jack fumbled with his pants on top of me. I was only sixteen, a mere baby, while Jack was a man, and knew what he was doing. Still, something had made me chuckle, to this day I can't remember what, but my laughter lit a fuse somewhere inside of Jack.

"What's wrong? Why are you laughing?" he asked. His long fingers worked feverishly to button up his pants.

"Oh, no, I'm not laughing at you!" The idea that I was laughing at him made me laugh harder. I was naked, and the folds of my 160 pound naked body shook and jiggled.

"What the hell?" He raised his voice as I laughed even harder.

Then it happened. He freaked out. He began to shake and gasp for air. His left leg started thumping the floor like a drummer missing his base pedal. He pounded on the windows with his fists.

"What's wrong?" I screamed.

"I'm dying…I'm dying." He kept repeating it, like I couldn't hear him.

"What do you mean?" My voice was high pitched. I was starting to panic.

"I'm DYING!" he screamed over and over.

I slid over to the driver side, threw my clothes on as fast as I could, and started the truck. "I will get you to the hospital," I promised him.

"No!" he yelled. He was dripping sweat. He was crying. He was shaking and fidgeting.

"JACK!" I yelled and grabbed him by the shoulders, "I will get you to a doctor."

"No. No." The shaking was starting to slow. He started to focus, to come back to earth.

I let him calm down for a good five minutes. Soon, he was still. He would not look at me. The space between us was large and partially lit by the moon overhead.

"What the fuck was that?" I asked. Was he on drugs? *Just my luck, I meet a nice guy and he has a coke habit.*

"It was nothing. Just take me home, please," he whispered. Outside, the river rushed in front of us. Other cars pulled up to the riverbank, hiding under the absence of street lights.

"We just had sex, I think you can tell me if you are on drugs or something."

"I'm not on drugs. I'm sick," he whispered.

"What kind of sick?" I asked. I remember thinking in that moment, *Please don't let him have cancer. Please don't let this be like Love Story and he will be dying in a bed like Ali McGraw while I plead for his life on the sidelines like Ryan O'Neal.*

"I have panic attacks," he stated. "I get them pretty bad, and pretty often. I just get really nervous and anxious. I can't control it. I'm sorry you had to see that. I just wanted you to enjoy this, and when you were laughing…well." He was suddenly a boy begging me with his bright blue eyes to help him, to make him feel okay.

"I'm sorry. I wasn't laughing at you. I was laughing at something in my head." I took his hands.

"Please don't break up with me. I'm sorry," he pleaded. We had only been dating three months.

I pulled Jack to my chest and ran my hands through his thick blond hair. We stayed that way for a long time. Sitting there in the silence with him plastered to my body made me feel warm and safe. I was needed, and as long as Jack needed me, he would never leave me. I belonged in that moment, in that embrace, in his disease. It was as if I had found a new home, a new cause to call my own. The cars came and went outside. The moon peaked out from behind a cloud then retreated again. Jack never let go, not for a minute. And just like that, our intimacy was born and we became wonderful lovers to one another. From the first time we had sex, to the very last time, our naked bodies next to one another always felt right.

With Ryan, it's different. There's nothing intimate between us. No shared feelings. No promises whispered into hot earlobes. It's 90% attraction and 10% something else. Like a fifteen year old, I'm still intoxicated by his smell, his smile, and his chuckle. My body tingles as I sit next to him. My skin explodes into goose bumps as he moves closer and his arm brushes mine. If I could make Ryan love me somehow, then I could forget about Jack and the fact that I wasn't good enough to keep him.

Suddenly, I summon all of my courage and lunge at Ryan like a starving dog. He is shocked. He slumps back into the couch under my weight. I run my tongue the length of his rough, rigid neck. My fingers fumble with his pants, but before I can unbutton them fully, he throws me onto my back and climbs on top of me. The Seinfeld credits roll from across the room. The inside of his mouth tastes like stale Marlboros and cheap beer. But his hands, they feel just right as they cross the plains of my squishy stomach and head north to my fleshy, un-toned breasts. The scruff on his face leaves red blotchy traces of where his mouth has been, like breadcrumbs, between my breasts, around my belly button, and finally the inside of my thighs.

When it is over, Ryan leaves me wrapped in a light green satin sleeping bag as he fumbles in the refrigerator for a beer.

"You want one, Amye?" he calls in from the kitchen.

"Yeah, sure."

Poor Ryan. He never sees it coming, the freight train of desperation heading his way. While he is in the next room digging for two cans of Budweiser, I am lying on his couch planning our future. Because it doesn't matter that the sex is not great. The emptiness inside of me, the hurt, the pain, the vast cavern of loneliness that Jack's leaving has opened up, needs to be filled. I cannot face more empty nights in my queen bed. I need a replacement, a band aid, something to stop the hurt. And food is no longer an option.

I am imagining how it will sound when Ryan whispers that he has fallen in love with me again. I am planning our wedding, picking out our children's names, and practicing my speech to his current children whom I will embrace as my own.

"You still have a mother, I am not here to replace your mommy," I would tell them as Ryan smiles and wraps his arms around my newly thin waist.

"Isn't she wonderful, kids?" he would gush and bury his head in my long, slender neck.

I imagine us bumping into Jack at the grocery store. Jack's eyes glossing over with regret as Ryan dips and kisses me passionately for the whole world to see, marking his territory. I imagine the phone calls, Jack on the other end, begging me to take him back. *Sorry Jack, really I am, but I'm happy now...* I would say. It would be my turn to hurt him, to choose someone else.

"Hey," Ryan comes back into the room interrupting my train of thought just as I am picking out our china pattern in my mind. "You better get dressed and go, I have work in the morning."

Chapter Seven

Losing weight is a lot like losing your mind. You are depriving your body of its most natural resource: food. Suddenly, that which you lack becomes the only thing you can think about, the only thing you see when you close your eyes. The key is, you cannot stay in one place for too long. Keep moving. Don't think about it. Walk everywhere, talk to strangers, take up the violin, or spend too much money. Do something, anything, to forget about the earthquake rumbling in the center of you, begging for nourishment.

Before my grandmother died, and after it became obvious that she would, she took to rocking. She could be anywhere: the doctor's, the mall, church, and eventually the Alzheimer's Unit of a nursing home. Anywhere with a place to sit down, you would find her swaying gently in the breeze. Her bright green eyes were far away and her small, thin lips were pressed tightly together as she wrapped her short chubby arms around her frail self and fell into a tick tock rhythm. This fascinated me on some level. What was she thinking about in those moments as the weight of her body swung back and forth like a pendulum? Now I realize. She was trying to forget that which she could still remember. It was easier than trying to make sense of it.

As I make my way around the 3.5 mile walking path circling Lake Scranton for the second time in the same day, I realize I am mimicking her: going in circles, staying in motion, trying to forget. It's a crisp Saturday morning and Georgia and I are walking briskly (according to my elevated pulse) along the curvaceous path, again. What Georgia doesn't know is that I've already been here this morning. I've already huffed and puffed my way along the paved path. I was afraid I would eat. It was either come here, or go to McDonalds.

Lake Scranton sits atop a mountain on Scranton's east side. It is a reservoir for most of the city, but for those of us who are trying to lose weight, it is our safe place. It is a place where you can exercise without having to step foot into a dreaded gym. Gyms are not a fat person's friend. In a gym there are thin people, judging stares, and hidden smirks. It's like walking into your high school prom all over again, except this time you really are naked, it's not just a nightmare. But here, among the snaking concrete road peppered with forest and breathtaking views of the water, you are almost invisible. Once in a while you will hear the clip clop of a runners shoes behind you, then in front of you, then fading into the trees in the distance. Once in a while you will get lapped by an old man wearing inappropriately short shorts which show off his bulging leg muscles. But for the most part, you are alone with your jiggling belly and squishy thighs.

"You know what I want to do when we lose the weight?" Georgia asks, her voice disappearing into the cold air. We do this almost every day, this game where we dream about ourselves as thin. It's the carrot we dangle.

"What?"

"I want to go to the beach. Just us," she says.

"Of course. Yeah, that would be fun," I say, winded from the slight incline under our feet. We have been walking this lake path everyday for the last month, to accelerate the process. We have it down to a science. We know which way to start (going left is easier, right has more hills), where all of the tough parts are, and exactly how long it will take us. Fifty one minutes is our record. We know that if we can complete the first mile within seventeen minutes, we may set a new record for ourselves.

"We won't tell anyone where we are going," Georgia says. Her thick brown hair is clipped together at the base of her neck by something that looks like a plastic piranha. Strands escape and fall against her chin as the cool fall wind lashes out at us.

"No way. And, whatever happens down there, stays down there. We won't breathe a word of it to anyone," I respond.

"We can act like total whores," Georgia says and her whole face lights up at the thought of being a slut at the beach.

"It will be our lost weekend," I say.

I can imagine us in our bikinis with bold boys doing belly shots off our washboard abs. I imagine neckties on doorknobs, awkward mornings, and splitting headaches. All of the things that skinny women get to enjoy that I have missed. Being skinny is a Utopia. A world with no problems. A world where men fall at your feet and send you flowers on a daily basis. Skinny is lovable. This is the mantra I repeat to myself in the darkness, with only the refrigerator light beckoning me to a package of cheese, or a leftover slice of pizza. *Skinny. Skinny.* It has been the unattainable for so long. Now, with Georgia's help, I have finally allowed myself to dream it into existence.

Georgia and I walk so close that occasionally our hips bounce off one another like ping pong balls. We are close. We are tight. We are pillars for one another to lean against. In the months that lie ahead, we will become one another's sponsors. Between us we will endure late night phone calls as fast food neon streams through our car windows, whispered bathroom panic over the presence of a dessert table as a bride and groom dance to an awful Celine Dion song somewhere outside, drunken slurring as we collectively try to count the points in ten beers. But through it all we will continue this walk. Through wind and rain, snow and sometimes sleet, we will climb this incline and sweat our way to the finish. Because this is our rocking. Our way to forget. Bad marriages, shitty jobs, and a deep, intense hunger. All of it will fall away like the pounds themselves.

Chapter Eight

Ryan won't return my calls. All sixteen of them. My fingers dial the number again, the number I know by heart. *Two three nine, four six six four.* Nothing, right to voicemail. That's number seventeen.

"Maybe you should give me the phone," suggests Stephanie, my coworker, and the latest witness to my desperation.

"No, fuck him. He's just ignoring me now," I slur.

It's happy hour, and I'm not happy. Me, Stephanie, and several other people from the local television station where I work are gathered at one of Scranton's many Irish pubs. McMillians, McGinty's, Finn McCools, everywhere you look there are Irish bars with blinking neon green signs in the windows. This establishment, The Banshee, is divided into little cubby holes filled with soiled couches, broken-in recliners, and funky little benches. Almost a recreation of Archie Bunker's living room in each nook. The gang from work flops themselves into the comfort of the washed out fabric seating, while I attach myself like a barnacle to the bar. Stephanie, noting my absence, has come to retrieve me.

I dial again. *Two three nine, four six six four*, that's eighteen.

"Maybe he's at work or something," Stephanie offers. Her long red-tinted blonde hair is poker straight and flows from the crown of her head like strawberry milk.

"For a week? Who works seven days straight?" I yell over the four guys wearing kilts that have just taken the stage in the restaurant area at our backs. The ceilings are tall and far away, so the music begins to bounce off the mahogany all around us. Outside the city is still clinging to its Christmas decorations, even though it's a week into the New Year. Reflections of red and green color the frosted windows like stained glass panels.

"Listen, Aim, you have to give this a rest. The guy is going to think you are crazy."

"I am crazy."

Two three nine, four six six four, that's nineteen.

"I know you like him but, Aim, really," Stephanie slugs from the sweating bottle in her left hand. Her eyes green lily pads, fix on mine.

"Okay. I'll stop calling. Right after this."

Two three nine, four six six four, that's twenty.

Ten minutes and one frosted mug of beer later, I'm slumped against a wood paneled partition staring at a group of professionals drinking imported beer, and I suddenly feel like I'm watching a commercial for the Gap. Ten people dressed in long fitted skirts or creased khakis and crisp white shirts chat about the latest sales figures, day care costs, and how their BMWs make whirring noises when they turn the wheel too hard to the left.

The truth is, for as far away as I feel from them right now, I love these people. They are my coworkers, my family for ten hours a day, five days a week. I spend more time with them than anyone else in my life. I love that Kim, the Local Sales Manager, lets us lock the office door at lunch and play Trivial Pursuit on her smooth oak desk. I love that Jen, the National Sales Manager, is a diehard Republican and sometimes turns the color of a Bing cherry when I bring up Bill Clinton's name. I love Patrick from Sales and his off-color humor. He once made a joke involving a baby and a coat hanger that brought gasps from everyone but me. I laughed so hard my stomach felt like a knot pulled tighter with every chuckle. And then there's Stephanie. The only other person my age. She and I first became friends when I was married to Jack and we were able to freely commiserate about our marriages. Now, she was just trying to prevent me from doing anything stupid. A full time job as of late.

I work in the traffic department at a local television station. What exactly happens in a traffic department you might ask? Well, we are the folks who decide in which order your commercials will play. We decide who gets the nice juicy internal spot in the middle of *CSI*, and who gets the much less desirable end break position. We are also responsible for playing the correct commercial copy as directed by the local advertising agencies. And finally, we are the people who take the orders from the sales department and enter them into the station's computers. What does this all mean? We control every advertisement you see.

I started working at WYOU, Scranton's CBS affiliate, when I was twenty years old, just two weeks after I graduated from Penn State. I had a Bachelor's degree in English, so it was either work in an office or go to graduate school. I chose the office. I started as an assistant, worked for a wonderful woman who took me under her wing and groomed me. When she left four years later to start a family, I was promoted to her job. Despite her best efforts, I was not ready. At twenty-four, I was the youngest Traffic Manager in the cluster of stations in our group. The day I was promoted, the only other person in my department walked off the job due to some sort of misplaced personal allegiance. I was alone and caught unprepared. The first three weeks I worked thirteen to fourteen hour days, just making sure there was *something* on the air. I made costly mistakes and learned on the fly. But after about six weeks, I had it. I began to like my job, and by all accounts, I was good at it.

In recent months, I have come to depend on this group of people like a family. The day I found out about Sarah, the other woman, I went straight into my boss's office. He was the first person I told. It was a Monday morning and Steve's head was buried in bright white papers illuminated by the fluorescents overhead. I started out composed:

Me: Hey, Steve, can we talk?

Him: Yes, Amye, what's up?

Me: Can I close the door?

He grows tense. Probably thinks I've figured out that I am grossly underpaid.

Him: Sure. *He lowers his reports and folds his thick fingers into one another.*

Me: Blah blah blah blah blah, my life is a mess, I just found out my husband has a girlfriend.

Him: *He releases his fingers and fans his palms over the pages in front of him.* Oh, I am so sorry. Take as much time as you need, honey.

In that moment, with Steve's calling me honey, his warm milk-chocolate eyes brimming with genuine concern, I lose it.

Me: Wah, wah, wah. *My tears fall thick and heavy like water balloons on his Berber carpet.*

Our office was sometimes like a pool of therapists available at any time. On any given day you could walk down the long row of cubicles and hear someone's life story being orated through sobs or chuckles. Sometimes there was a gathering, a cluster of people ready to doll out amateur advice. Other times, it was a low whispered one on one, like a narrative hum emanating from a partially opened door.

We know everything about each other. I know Angie's daughter keeps having kids out of wedlock. Maria's husband works long hours and she worries he might end up neglecting her and their children. Sue's boyfriend is dragging his feet with a commitment, despite the fact that she has practically given up her youth waiting for him to marry her. And, likewise, they know everything about me. They know I was married to a man who couldn't leave the house. They know Jack and I are in the process of a divorce and that he is sleeping with Sarah, his boss. Of all of them, Stephanie knows me the best. She has spent countless hours in my office listening to and watching the slow-motion deterioration of my marriage.

Jack and I did not fall apart overnight. I did not fall asleep one night in a blissful marriage, only to wake up the next day in misery. I imagine it was more like watching a rock climber descend down a large smooth cliff while dangling by a rugged nylon thread. We would fall, steady ourselves, and plummet some more. We had a cycle: Jack did something bizarre, I overreacted, and then we made up. But the breaks, the cracks in the cliff were growing larger and further apart. It was becoming increasingly difficult to straddle the gap. We had only been married for two years, but our relationship was on shaky ground for years before we even walked down the aisle. In fact, six weeks before the wedding, Jack had passed out drunk on the couch with a lit cigarette. If I had not woken up to the intense smell permeating our apartment, he or I would have been dead.

I called off the wedding and moved out the next day, into my current apartment. But the break, my resolve, it didn't last long. After only two days, the ritual began. Jack, at my new door drenched in a sadness so heavy his skin looked to be melting from his bones, begging my forgiveness. It was his disease, he said. He didn't know how to control it so he was drinking it away. He needed me. He needed my strength. He needed, he needed, he needed. It never occurred to him to change one of those verbs to "wanted." But I, convinced he would fall apart if I left him for real, stared into his swimming pool blue eyes and saw the same boy I made love to in the cab of a truck so many years ago. The same boy who needed me then, still needed me. And before I could crawl out from under the weight of that need, I was tethered back, into forgiveness.

With Ryan, however, it just ends. And now, in this Irish bar where the music is creating a bubble around me and I have to scream to pierce its outer membrane, I am trying to hang on to whatever is left between us. Stephanie means well as she wrestles my hot-pink covered cell phone from my sweaty grip.

"Give it to me now," she orders through clenched teeth. Around us the parade of yuppies chat about summer cottages, car leases, and trips to Disneyworld. I tighten my grip on the phone, even though I know that Stephanie can run my life one hundred times more efficiently than I can at this point.

"You cannot be trusted," she leans in and announces loudly.

"I know."

She's right. I am being devoured by pain. The hole in my heart is a long hallway begging to be paced; it's where I live. In the two weeks that have passed since Ryan and I first had sex on his living room couch, I have been trying to mold him into my life. To plug him into the void left by Jack.

I forced my help on him, even though he didn't need it. I invited him for dinner with my family, even though we weren't dating. I bought him presents for Christmas, and when he wouldn't commit to seeing me within a week's time of the date, I drove by his house and left them on the seat of his truck. I brought to his house a soggy bag of Burger King before he left for work one day, and pretended not to notice the strange stare on his face as he took the food but didn't invite me in. I was convinced he needed to be fixed, I just couldn't seem to find the break.

Then, the final nail in the coffin came last week: New Year's Eve. After drinking with my mother and her friends all night at a local hotel bar, I decided to drive to his house, despite his not answering the phone (again), and despite his previous announcement that he would be with his children and could not see me. Still, I drove to his house, and when he wasn't home I sat on his steps and waited. The whole time I held a beer bottle in my hands, like a homeless woman.

A few of Ryan's neighbors took pity on me and invited me in for a drink, but they were underage and soon a mother in a towel headdress and floral muumuu threw me out onto the street, threatening to call the police. When Ryan arrived home, with his kids, I was passed out on his front porch. He barely spoke to me as he dragged me into the backseat of his car and drove me home.

It was all too much. He had warned me: he had sons, three of them, and he wasn't available the way most men were. But I didn't want to listen. I didn't want to admit that yet another man might be rejecting me.

"Give me the phone, Amye," Stephanie demands.

Before I loosen my grip, I dial one last time: *Two three nine, four six six four.* Nothing.

"Okay, here," I whisper and surrender my stronghold.

And just like that, Ryan is gone.

Chapter Nine

Days later, I am climbing onto a scale at Weight Watchers. I am one in a line of hopeful women, clinging to the possibility of the clunky black weight sliding farther to the left than last week. I have heard that hope and optimism are two different things. Hope is *wanting* good things to happen. I *want* to lose weight. I *want* to be skinny. I *want* to fall in love with a man who adores me, get married on the beach wearing a thin, spaghetti-strapped gown, honeymoon on the Riviera, feel my belly swell with new life, and write poetry that falls onto bookshelves. That's hope.

Optimism is more evidence based. It is the act of expecting good things to happen based on the evidence that shows good things have already occurred, therefore they can keep occurring. I am optimistic that when my small, wide feet step onto a paper towel on top of a black square, that a rectangular, metal weight will slide easily to the left, because that's what has been happening for the past five months. I am optimistic that I will be able to purchase size ten jeans someday soon, based on the fact that my jean sizes have slid from twenty four to sixteen in only a few months.

Nervous Joan with the shaky hands is optimistic as well. "Wow, Amye, you are just disappearing before my eyes. Another 3.5 pounds this week." She flips through the tri-folded cardboard record of my weight, "You'll be at your goal in no time!"

*Oooh*s and *aaah*s muddle in from the line of women behind me.

Most stand with their shoes and any extraneous clothing already off. In the winter the kind women who run this show keep the heat at seventy-eight, to accommodate those of us who dress like it is July outside.

"You must feel like a million bucks," a woman in line says as I walk past her.

"I do," I answer back.

"I wish I could lose that much," she says as she takes her two hands, grabs the fat in her belly that hangs over her nylon shorts, and gives it a jiggle.

"You will," I tell her, "You just have to have hope."

At the group meeting after the weigh in, Pantsuit Pam talks about our self image. I sit quietly and rub my hands along the tops of my legs. They are starting to narrow, transforming from tree trunks to thick branches.

"We live in a society that, unfortunately, does not tolerate obesity well," Pantsuit Pam tells the twelve or thirteen of us who have opted to stay for her lecture. "But you have to remember that you are in charge of how you feel. The image that you have of yourself is the most important. What do you think about yourselves?"

"Not much," Sherri (with an i) blurts out.

Pantsuit Pam whips around like a tornado. "Not much? Who said that?"

Sherri raises her paw into the air.

"Sherri, explain. Why don't you feel like much?"

"Well, my husband left me for another man. That hurt. And my coworkers make fun of my weight behind my back," Sherri says. She's a beautiful girl, one of those heavy women that us fat girls refer to as a "permanent." She's been fat probably for most of her life, causing her features to grow naturally to that size. This simply means that she looks pretty, fat. Then there's people like me, who get fat suddenly. When you take a thin person and pump 100 pounds of air into them, their features distort. You can always spot those people: the freakishly thin limbs, narrow nose, small chin with seven new ones bursting out behind it. It's not very pretty.

"Sherri, all of those things you just told me are coming from someone else. I didn't ask what your husband or your coworkers think of you, I asked what *you* think of yourself."

"I…I..I dunno. I guess I'm okay," Sherri mutters.

Pantsuit Pam walks to a folding table at the back of the room. *Click, click, click.* The five fluorescent lights hanging overhead change her green pantsuit to a deep blue.

"Here. Take this," she orders Sherri, handing her a hand-mirror, "Now I want you to look at yourself and say three nice things."

Sherri stares at the reflection and her eyes well up with tears. From where I sit, on her right, I can hear her breathing quicken, puffs of self-consciousness escaping from her lungs. I look around the room. The other women are watching her intently. Sherri is the one with the mirror, but we are all standing there with her, just like we do every day at home. Naked, in front of the mirror, searching for the pretty girl who used to live in our bodies.

"I guess I have nice eyes," she mutters. The group claps. "And my lips are a good shape." The group claps louder. "I have a pretty face," Sherri says loudly. "I'm pretty."

The room erupts in sobs and applause. Several jump from their seats and wrap their arms like a cocoon around Sherri. Pantsuit Pam has done the impossible: She has made a room of fat girls feel pretty.

On the drive home, I try to remember the last time I felt pretty. As a young girl, nine or ten years old, I had confidence in spades. I was popular in school, had my pick of the boys, and numerous admirers. But that ended, and until Pantsuit Pam brought it to my attention, I never really revisited the year that changed my life. The year that I went from having evidence-based optimism to having unrealistic hope.

The year is 1989. I fall in love for the first time in the fall. I am thirteen and the leaves are fading under my feet. I still listen to men in makeup with high hair singing about *Girls, Girls, Girls.* On the bus ride home from school one November afternoon, I meet a boy, let's call him Oliver, and we start dating. Ollie is older, he's a whopping fifteen years old, and comes from a broken home, the *really* broken kind where Dad is gone and Mom is in a hospital for depression. The kind where car parts lie on the kitchen table and curtains are just blankets thumb-tacked over the windows. Ollie's had to grow up quick and depends on no one. He takes good care of me, brands me with his mark and makes sure no one even looks at me the wrong way. He beats up the boys who ask me out, threatens the girls who bully me, and shrouds me in a blanket of safety.

We see each other at school and for a few hours after, if I can manage a lie convincing enough to buy me some time out of the house. Band practice, violin practice, cheerleading tryouts, student council; I use anything I can think of to give Ollie and me a few hours of groping one another on the tan couch in his basement. My mother begins to grow suspicious of my sudden love for extracurricular activities. On Ollie's basement couch, Ozzy Osbourne provides the background music. Ollie throws an old Superman sleeping bag over us in case one of his older brothers comes down the loose wooden stairs. We are lumps of clay under that blanket, squeezing and squishing one another into various positions.

Months go by and Ollie successfully convinces me to sleep with him. The preparations are minimal: a condom, a copy of Ozzy's *Goodbye to Romance* in the form of a cassette tape, and a single red candle (even though it's daylight). It's a Saturday and I am supposed to be at Georgia's house. Instead, I am flat on my back with Ollie on top of me. *Does it hurt?* he whispers over Ozzy's metallic voice. It's over in five minutes and I don't feel like I should, like everyone has promised: closer, more in love, bonded, mature, connected. I feel the same as I did before- insanely in love with this boy.

My family takes a trip to Ocean City, Maryland, where I buy an airbrushed T-Shirt that says, *Amye loves Ollie*. I wear it all summer. At a slumber party with my girlfriends, I carve his initials into my ankle, where they remain twenty years later. I spend hours lying on my parents' brass bed, connected to the corded phone with Ollie's soft voice on the other end.

Then it begins to go awry. Ollie begins to fall in with an older crowd, people his own age. Together they spend their evenings alongside the Lackawanna River and huff spray paint. With their heads floating, they walk into the contaminated river, they swim, they laugh, they fondle loose girls with no parental restrictions.

Ollie breaks up with me on a warm spring night after school. I jog down the three steps from the bus and find him waiting for me. He has since quit school and spends most of his days working on cars, something he will eventually make a career of. My smile turns flat when he says the words. *I don't want you anymore.* Despite ransacking my memory I cannot now recall the specific reason. Was it another girl? Throughout the ping-ponging back and forth over the following decade, there will be many other girls. But was this the start of it? Was the initial break because of infidelity? I can't remember the details, but I remember the fallout.

The crying is intense. It's produced far down in my gut and wrenches the whole works on the way up to my throat. I spend days walking around like a zombie, crying at the drop of a hat, avoiding friends and family. As a teenager, heartbreak has a way of sending me into solitary confinement, unlike today when I cannot stand being alone for one split second. Ozzy plays on my stereo nonstop. In school, I write *Amye loves Oliver* a billion times, covering tablets, books, desk tops, anything with a flat surface. I retrace the initials carved into my ankle. I call Ollie three, four times a day, begging for a chance to talk. He hangs up on me.

That's how I end up alone in my bedroom with a different boy on top of me. The average fourteen-year-old boy weighs about one hundred and twenty-five pounds. This boy feels like four or five sacks of potatoes, so I guess that's about average. The only comparison I have is Ollie, but he's small, much more compact. A few days earlier, news had come of this boy wanting to date me, to pick up what Ollie discarded and make something from it. This new boy, Drew, is the cutest boy in school, long hair, rock t-shirts, a wonderful broad smile and happens to be a good friend of Ollie's. I accepted, hoping jealousy would draw Ollie back to me.

Drew asks to come into my room one Saturday afternoon while my parents are gone. I agree to let him in, but there is something brewing in the center of me, a spark of some kind, a fire trying to ignite, a smoke signal of danger ahead. In my room I have one window, which overlooks a busy highway. Sometimes, I forget that highway is there, the noise of it having faded into the background of my life. But with this boy on top of me it is suddenly loud and intrusive.

I said *yes*, at first, agreeing to let him climb on top of me after he assured me that such an act would help with the heartbreak, increase my popularity, cement him as my boyfriend. Then, as the tractor trailers and motorcycles invade our intimacy, my answer switches to *no*. *No*, I say again. He cannot hear me. The window is open, the traffic is raging like a steam engine outside. *No*, I say. *I'm almost done*, he whispers through clenched teeth.

Please no. I wiggle my arms from his grip, his long thin fingers like serpents around my wrists.

Shut up.

I changed my mind.

Shut up.

Afterwards, my wrists are red and my thighs are gooey from his release. My bed is small and shoved up against the popcorn plaster wall, I roll into the corner. With tears streaming down my face I cannot look at this boy as he pulls up his pants and leaves. Ten minutes after Drew has cleared out and I have composed myself, my phone lights up, the pink neon blinking a hot red. It's Drew's friend. "Drew doesn't want to go out with you anymore, you fucking whore." Dead air.

Almost immediately the event becomes foggy. A haze moves into my memory and will stay there for twenty years. *Did I say no? Did I say yes?* The next day at school, I discover that Drew has told everyone about our afternoon. Everyone including Ollie. Ollie hates me now. *How could you?* he screams in my face at the bus stop after school. I try to answer, to connect the fragments in my head and string them from my mouth to his ears in a cohesive, rational way, but I can't.

"He was on top of me, and I told him no," I whimper. A crowd has gathered around us now. It is late in the school year, one of the last days. Everyone is casual, everything is untucked.

"Did you or did you not sleep with him?"

"I did, but not because I wanted to."

"Did you let him into your bedroom?" Ollie's voice trembles with anger.

"Yes. But I didn't know…" I cannot convince him. All I can do is cry.

"You're a fucking whore!" Ollie isn't mad anymore, he's actually smiling, laughing. Proud of himself that he can puff out his chest and call a woman a whore in front of his friends.

"Please, Ollie, please, just listen, I didn't know what was happening," I sob, publicly. I move towards him and grab for his shirt.

"Get away from me." He jumps away. He spits on the ground at my feet and walks away.

My social life is destroyed. At school I become a whore and a slut. Drew never talks to me again, except to tell me that his new girlfriend wants me dead. I avoid said new girlfriend like the plague. I stay in at night, I miss every school football game or gathering, I finally tell my parents and spend a few months in therapy where I learn to say the word "rape," as in *date* rape, but it doesn't help.

Ollie tries to forgive me, sleeps with me, loves me again for weeks at a time, until he inevitably remembers my betrayal and leaves me crying in the street, on the bus, in the halls at school. He ridicules me publicly, tells any new friend I make what I have done. Then, under the cover of night, when his guard has dropped again, he cradles me into his chest while we sob together. Ollie's other best friend, Timmy, is the only person who listens to me. We become confidants, friends, spending hours on the phone discussing what had happened. But we can never see one another in the light of day. Timmy's leniency towards me is a betrayal to Ollie, and soon our friendship is cut short as well.

I am fourteen and I am already ruined. I cry constantly, I slip into a period of self loathing that is the most intense I have ever felt. I hide from the world, staying home with food as my only comfort, turning down social invitations for fear of public humiliation. I think of ways to kill myself. I swallow ten pills, then twelve, then stop. Thoughts of my mother, my father, Jennie, strong enough to tether me to this earth a little while longer. I begin writing poetry. It saves my life.

Years later, when I told Jack this story on a warm summer night on a grassy hill overlooking the city, he believed me, no questions asked. He pulled me onto his lap, cradled me in his arms, and together we became a lake, still and calm. I married him because of that.

That was it; that was the moment I stopped feeling pretty. The moment when I began to depend on other people's opinions to define myself. Ollie thought I was a liar, a slut, a no-good piece of trash. Drew thought I was easy, stupid, foolish. I told myself *I must be these things*, since most of my peers agreed. From that point on, I was damaged goods. The seal was broken, the contents had been disturbed. From then on, it was a matter of finding someone who would accept the defective product I had become. That one sucker who wouldn't care that I was some form of used up. And here I was, all of these years later, still repeating the same pattern. Begging Ryan to accept me, even though he is far from what I would ever want in a new relationship. I will settle, because no one else will want me. I have no optimism, because I have no evidence to tell me otherwise.

Chapter Ten

Yesterday is just that…over. This is what I tell myself every day. It's a lesson I'm working hard to learn, and every morning the mistakes of the day before are gone, erased. Each day is a clean slate: no bad decisions have been made, no tears have been shed, and no anger has swelled like an ocean at high tide. Today I will forget that Jack ever existed, that he is still seeing Sarah. I will forget that I hate my job so much I want to cry. I will forget that the first man who even looked at me since my separation refuses to take my calls. *I will be strong today, no crying.* I will stay within my points, OP, as us Weight Watcher's people call it: On Program. *I will harness my inner strength, every little bit of it, and I will not break. Not today.*

Then, as I'm hopping in my car to drive to work, I hear an Indigo Girl's song that reminds me of Jack, the two of us at sixteen, so young and in love with nothing but our future ahead of us. I remember how it felt when our relationship was fresh and new, before everything soured. I become so filled with hurt and anger that I want to drive to Jack's house and destroy it with a nuclear missile. Instead, I hit the drive thru at McDonald's and order a sausage McMuffin with egg and a chocolate milkshake, 22 points.

Afterwards, with the greasy food rumbling around in my belly, I think about what I've done and want to puke. I want to cry, hit something, drown myself, whatever will make the remorse dissipate. I have once again given in to my urge, the obsession, a force controlling the very center of me. This is the face of food addiction. We promise, we disappoint, we eat, we feel bad, we repeat. It's a daily struggle for metabolic sobriety. A vicious cycle of self-sabotage. This is why I need Pantsuit Pam to help me break the cycle.

Later in the week at Weight Watchers, Pantsuit Pam asks us to think about the first time in our lives that we felt fat. The very first time that weight was pitch-forked into the front of our consciousness. I shift my weight from left to right, my ass cheeks numbing from the cool metal under me. Above us five fluorescent lights hum and buzz, reflected in the shiny tile under our feet. Next to me a large woman with holes for dimples and tree trunks for legs stands up and tugs at her floral muumuu. She has two tone hair, a lovely, deep brown with brittle gray snaking over the top.

"It was the first summer I went to camp," she blurts out, like this is something that has been brewing in her subconscious for years, just waiting for Pantsuit Pam to come along and pluck it out. "I was seven and all of the other girls were wearing bikinis. I thought I could too, so I made my mother buy me a stars and stripes two piece. Oh, don't get me wrong," she turns to the rest of us in the circle around her, "it was still very modest. But the other girls, they ridiculed me. They pushed me into an inner tube and sent me floating into the middle of the lake. They called me a whale and laughed."

"Angela," Pantsuit Pam moves towards her and grabs her hand, "I'm so sorry that you experienced that cruelty. How did you feel after camp? When you left those girls?"

"I was never the same," Angela says through the shaking sobs sitting in the back of her throat.

A few more people volunteer to share their shame, to rip apart their memories searching for the one, the culprit, the tricky little bastard that started it all. Ginger from Greenridge remembers being fifteen and losing her virginity to a guy on the football team. She felt like big shit, like the queen bee. Then, the next day at school it was revealed that the boy only slept with Ginger because he felt bad for her, she was such a loser. The pity fuck. I immediately think of Ryan, of the sex on his dirty futon. I think of the way he looked at me when I told him my husband had left me for another woman, or when I complained about how slow the weight loss was going. How he shoved me away from him afterwards, always. *Oh my God, was I a pity fuck?*

Next up is Cheryl. She wasn't fat until she had her first baby. She was always a size six, prided herself on her tight ass and flat stomach. But, it's been four years since the baby was born and the once flat stomach is now hanging to the floor. Cheryl hasn't seen her feet in four years and three months, she has it down almost to the day. Her husband has stopped sleeping with her, has moved his skinny ass onto the fold-out couch in his home office. Now, the kid sleeps with her, loves her for who she is. Cheryl's voice cracks when she talks. She is a beautiful woman, only my age, maybe a little older. Her big blonde hair is plush with chunky curls, the kind I would die for. She's not even that fat, she's maybe a size fourteen. Once you've been a size twenty-eight, fourteen is a pretty low number.

I never knew what was making me fat; I only had memories, glimpses of times in my life where I felt exceptionally skinny or substantially overweight. I remember being twelve and going on a school field trip to the Anthracite Coal Mine Tour. Without my parents' knowing it, I had slipped into a low cut shirt that allowed the boys on the bus a glimpse of my growing breasts. An hour later I felt the sun on my chest as Jamie Moran and I felt each other up like dogs in heat behind the Anthracite Gift Shop.

Next, I'm fifteen and my Grandfather has just died. My mother hems and haws as I struggle to squeeze both my oversize chest and my ballooning hips into a black, size thirteen dress. I do not remember this, I'm only reminded years later by a photograph. In the still image, I'm standing outside a local restaurant, sullen, the mark of shame on my face as I shyly turn away from the camera, hiding my body. *It was starting already, the camouflaging.* Jennie is seventeen and stands next to me in a size two mini dress.

Fast forward and I am twenty-four, about to be married. I'm

standing at the back of a church and it is breathtakingly beautiful. It's a night time ceremony and the whole church is lit by candles. On the stairs of the altar there are brushed silver lanterns with stars cut out of the top. The ceilings are high and angular, there is a sky full of stars above our heads. I should be filled with pride, remembering the ten months it took for me to plan this night. I should be bursting with happiness that I am marrying Jack, the man I have loved for the past eight years. I should be thinking about our future. I should be thinking about a lot of things. Instead, my head is ratcheted backwards three hours to a small room at Jennie's house, where I am stuffed into my size twenty-eight wedding dress like a beach ball being squeezed into a book bag. I cannot forgive myself for this.

And this is how my weight gain happens. A timeline of images, a melody of misery. My weight is a song and trying on dresses seems to be the chorus, repeating over and over. There is no memory of the *first* moment; it has been erased by a lifetime of dreaming of what it would be like to be skinny. Skinny was something that was never attainable, a place I could never exist. The golden land of milk and honey, where boys fell all over you and treated you like a princess, where you were promoted easily because you were pretty, where you never had to pay a bill or skip a meal. Skinny was always the answer to my problems, the one thing that would make everything better. It was everything I ever wanted.

Chapter Eleven

On a cold afternoon in January, just days before the big move at work, Jennie informs me that she is doing some moving of her own. We are in a hot tub, finishing a bottle of red wine when she announces she's moving to New York City. The words trickle from her mouth like the last drops of syrup from an overturned bottle. They are thick, muddy, slow, unsure.

"What?" I ask. The jets on our back create a vacuum of white noise around us.

"We're moving to New York," she mutters, barely audible.

"What?" My lip starts to shake at the thought of my only sister being so far away.

"Amye, please, don't be upset," Jennie says as she swirls the remaining red puddle against the insides of her long-stemmed glass.

The "we" is her and her fiancée, Josh. They met shortly after Jennie's breakup with her high school boyfriend and have been dating ever since. That was almost ten years ago. Josh is a wonderful man; my family, myself included, loves him. But the truth is, he and Jennie are artists, and they're having a hard time finding work in small town Scranton.

"When?" I ask, not trying to hide the tears flowing down my cheeks and disappearing as they hit the steaming water.

"Soon. March 1st."

"But that's only a few months away."

A gray, bleak sky hangs over us like an empty canvas. Jennie and I provide the only colors in the landscape. We are on the back deck of Josh's mother's house, doing what we do on Sunday afternoons drinking wine and soaking in a hot tub. I can have two glasses of wine only. (eight points). We started this ritual a few weeks ago, when Jennie realized Sundays were the loneliest days for me to spend tooling around an empty apartment. It was designed to be a distraction.

"I can't believe you're leaving," I say through actual sobs.

"Aim...please. Don't cry. You're gonna be okay, Dad is here."

The truth is, I'm not surprised. I've known since a young age that Jennie was not meant for this town. She has been an artist for as long as I have known her, since the age of three, and she wasn't going to give it up anytime soon. It's something I've always envied about her: she has had her whole career mapped out in front of her since that age, and never wavered. Jennie was going to chase her dream, to follow her path to the mecca of artistic energy.

I, on the other hand, was always a writer, but never gave it the attention it deserved. In fact, I never even considered writing professionally until I was in high school, when a few words from a teacher changed how I thought about my poetry. I started writing as a reaction, a response to stimuli, when I was eleven and stumbled upon a riveting episode of Sally Jesse Raphael after school one day. Sally, in her signature red glasses, circled on the small stage around a young girl and her parents, all in lush white leather chairs. The young girl was claiming that her stepfather had abused her several times over the past year. While Sally and the audience sat motionless, the girl's mother began to confront the man, begging for the truth. It wasn't long before the seriousness with which Sally and her producers approached the subject was gone, the confrontation quickly diminishing to a "he said, she said" battle, with the mother as neutral as Switzerland. I, however, was moved by this show and this young girl who looked as if she was my age. I wrote my first poem later that night:

The Dark Room

The dark room is my own special place I can hide,
I go to the dark room cause I feel safe inside
often I sit in the dark room and cry,
as I watch under the door for his feet to pass by.

He is my nightmare, my bad dreams come true,
He is the one who makes my skin black and blue.
I can't cry for help, cause he says it's my sin,
So I go to the dark room where he can't get in.

Swollen and bruised my eye releases a tear,
as I sit in the dark room shaking from fear.
My hands start to shake, something's not right...
Suddenly out went the dark, and in came the light.

When I finished I emerged from my bedroom holding my masterpiece, ready to show it to any and all available audiences. Like a new mother, naive to the concept of contamination, I pulled my baby around by its ear and showed it to everyone I knew.

"Amye!" my mother gasped as she sat at the kitchen table holding the sheet of paper. I sat across from her with my chin resting in my hands, waiting for the moment when a proud smile would wash across her face. "This is…" she muttered. It was working. I could see the pain and horror in her eyes as she felt the same bond with this young girl that I had felt. My mother must have read that poem ten times before lowering the paper just enough to see my face, smiling and patiently waiting for her praise. "What would make you write something like this?" she asked.

My father, an artist himself, was thrilled on the other hand that I was showing some artistic promise and took pride in my work. He loved the poem, and when Sparrowgrass Poetry Forum agreed to publish it for the low, low price of fifty dollars, he not only gave me the cash but lacquered a copy of the acceptance letter onto a plaque and hung it on the wall in the living room. My mother refused to acknowledge its existence, and to this day stares at my Uncle Joe with suspicion.

"The Dark Room" incident helped me to realize that I could write, but it wasn't until I was a senior in high school that someone actually took my writing seriously. After submitting several creative writing pieces to my Senior English teacher, Mrs. Langan, a woman I greatly respected if for nothing else but her passionate portrayal of Lady Macbeth's hand-scrubbing scene, pulled me aside one day after class.

"Amye, great job on these," she said as she handed me back my stack of writing, "I'm really a big fan of your work." And that was it. She changed the path of my life with those words. I have been writing ever since, all because of that comment.

Now, I was losing my sister to her calling.

"More?" Jennie's glass clanks against the fiberglass tub as she pours another glass for herself. She is wearing a bikini, something I will never be able to do. Her long, wet hands shake in the cold air, causing some wine to spill in the water. Suddenly we look like extras in a *Jaws* movie.

"Sure," I answer and hold out my glass.

"I'm sorry, Aim. Please, don't be mad." Jennie's nose scrunches up and her back stands long and tall when she gets defensive.

"I'm not, Jen."

I melt into forgiveness when I see her lips trembling. I think of my father, a promising artist who gave it all up to raise us at only twenty years old. I think of my own resentment and how I was stuck in Scranton for the last ten years because Jack would never even consider moving. I don't want Jennie to feel stuck here tending to her heartbroken sister. I know how it feels to have a part of you that you can't close off. I know how it feels to want to succeed in your craft, to be noticed, and to be inspired. I can't rob Jennie of that. Even if it means we will be living two hours away from one another. Even if it means losing another piece of home.

Chapter Twelve

Jennie's moving is just another line added to the list of things spinning wildly out of my control. *I don't get it*, I say to Georgia as we reach the first mile marker on the path around Lake Scranton. It's cold, very cold. We're dressed in sweatpants and sweatshirts, hats and scarves. But the bitter wind biting at our backs does not deter us from the journey. *I'm doing everything right, I'm down forty pounds, and still, nothing is getting better.* Georgia glances at me, taking her eyes off the path briefly, *skinny people have problems too, you know*, she says.

I want to ask Georgia about *her* problems. About the dead-end marriage in which she is stuck, about the addictions that have snaked their way into her family, but I can't. Georgia is the complete opposite of me. She is like a vault: everything goes in, and nothing comes out. Every so often she cracks, and her pain will rise to the surface just long enough for me to remember it's there, before she pushes it back down and locks it away. She has been that way ever since I've known her.

Georgia and I met in Miss Helen's ballet class when we were five years old. It was a weekly class, every Tuesday 4-5 pm, and our participation was more to appease our parents than anything else. One afternoon, a few young girls were running through the curtain that separated the changing area from the lobby. They giggled as the heavy cotton clung to their scalps, revealing their red, shiny faces only after they ran the length of the doorway. I decided to join in while my mother paid her bill, thus turning her back and allowing me five minutes of mischief.

While I ran through the curtain one way, Georgia ran through the other, and what resulted was a head-on collision. I ended up with a concussion, relegated to lying on the couch and resting for days, which to a five-year-old is on par with torture, while Georgia escaped completely unscathed. She simply stood up, dusted herself off, and went on with her life. It is that strength, that ability to dust herself off and move on, that I both love and envy in her. We remained best friends for many years, until a menial fight over a boy drove a division between us. And not just any boy, Jack.

Georgia was with me the night I met Jack, the night I fell head over heels in love with him. She joined me when my patience ran thin waiting for him to call, and I decided to stalk him. Literally. We had two pieces of information: he lived in Taylor, and he was a volunteer fireman. So naturally we climbed into Georgia's 1993 Chevy Lumina, drove to the only firehouse in Taylor, parked in the very back of the parking lot and waited. When Jack emerged we followed him home. Now we had an address. This went on for two or three nights until his voice on the other end of my phone finally parachuted me to sanity.

Over the next few months, hell years, I poured all of my time and attention into Jack and our relationship, leaving my friendship with Georgia to disintegrate and fade away. I wasn't there when she was married. I wasn't there when her son was born. Important moments that I should have been a part of. Then, one random night in June, a few years later, she called. She needed me. She was miserable and sad. She was scared and alone. We both were. She had felt betrayed by her husband, hurt by his lies, only unlike me now, she didn't have the proof she needed to tear her family apart. She had a child to think of. We've been helping one another through bad marriages ever since. Now, I couldn't imagine my life without her.

These walks around the lake keep us close. Our lives are on such different paths right now, that it would be easy for me to orbit away from her like I have in the past. But when we are on this path together, two soldiers marching against the army of heft, we are united. We spill our secrets, dream our futures, and imagine our bodies shrinking. This walk is as important to our hearts as it is to our thighs. It is our time.

On the way home I am reminded of that ride to the movies so many years ago. The way we reconnected without missing a beat. Georgia still drives too fast and too close to other cars, and I still hang on for dear life, as she weighs the pros and cons of leaving her marriage.

"You know what Gram always says, Georgia," I remind her.

"I know. 'When you've had enough, you'll know it'," Georgia repeats.

"Well have you?" It's the same conversation. The same words that ping ponged between us that night. Only I've gotten out. Not by choice, maybe, but I'm free nonetheless. Now, I'm setting a shitty example for the benefits of that decision. I'm drowning my misery in beer and boys. I'm crying at night because I can't stand not feeling a living, breathing body next to mine when I roll over in bed. I'm consumed by anger, fixated on Jack and Sarah, and how to bring them down. Instead of focusing on the fact that Jack is not my husband anymore, I should be relishing the fact that Jack is not my *problem* anymore.

"I don't know, Aim. I really don't. I don't want to break my family apart," Georgia's eyes are far away. She clicks on the radio and we don't say another word.

I am ashamed of myself. I'm telling her to leave her husband, to take her child and start a new life alone, and I can't even handle that decision myself. I need to be stronger. I need to show Georgia that being alone isn't the end of the world. But from where I'm sitting, that inner peace feels like it's a million miles away.

part two

Chapter Thirteen

The day I am finally able to execute my revenge plan happens upon me by accident. I am hiding behind a cheap display of personalized pet clothes in the middle of the Viewmont Mall watching Sarah, *the* Sarah, eat a slice of pizza in the food court with a person I have deduced from my Facebook research must be her sister.

"What should I do?" I whisper into my cell phone. Suddenly the dialogue I had been writing in my head for months has slipped away.

"Go say something," Stephanie says, "You know I would."

"But what can I say?"

"Are you kidding me? Call her a home wrecking whore, tell her off."

"I can't do that," I admit.

"Do you need me to come up there? I'll get in my car right now."

"I'll call you back," I whisper and hang up.

Although my legs are shaking with terror, I am a blend of emotions. I have been fantasizing about this moment for so long. I had envisioned this in my brain a million times. In my fantasy, it goes something like this:

Me, at my goal weight, dressed in a bikini and a mini skirt, for absolutely no reason, walking into RadioShack to purchase a new phone. Sarah, now fifty pounds heavier since dating Jack and subsisting mostly on a diet of Burger King and McDonalds, standing behind the counter forced to wait on me, to satisfy my consumer needs.

Sarah! I almost didn't recognize you, I would announce as I flip through a huge stack of hundred dollar bills to pay for my phone. She would say something back like *Oh life with Jack is so fantastic*. But the look in her eyes will tell me that she is sorry, so sorry, and she wishes she could return him, like a broken television. Then, as I'm getting ready to leave, I'd spin around to discover Jack standing behind me. *He's* fifty pounds heavier also, oh, and bald. *Oh Jack! What a surprise!* I would say as I flip my hair over my left shoulder like I did the night we met, an action he told me months later he thought was sexy. As I begin to leave, he grabs my thin arm and whispers in my ear: *I love you, take me back, you look gorgeous.*

That was how it was supposed to go down. But it was supposed to happen months from now, when I was happy again, further along in my weight loss, and dating a terrific man. Not now. I'm not ready. But then I spot a GameStop bag on the floor next to her, surely containing something for Jack, and as Sarah giggles and tosses *her* perfectly straight blonde hair over *her* left shoulder, I want to explode in a fit of rage. Like a steam engine, a fire is building in the belly of me. I am not in charge of my actions anymore. Some dark force has taken over. *How dare she sit there eating a slice of (delicious looking) pizza, like everything is hunky-dory in the world, while I deal with the scraps of dignity to which she has left me clinging. And who the fuck only orders one slice of Roma's Pizza, anyway?*

Before I can plot out my strategy, an annoying salesman rounds the corner of the wooden partition where I've been hiding.

"Hello, Ma'am, would you like to see our collection of personalized doggy pillows?"

"Uh, no thanks," I mutter and move out into the open. Now, I am like a deer in headlights. I know Sarah can see me. We are only twenty feet away from one another at most. My feet start moving towards her, almost by themselves. This is it. I'm headed straight for her. Fifteen feet... *What am I going to say? What if I punch her? Will the mall security guards arrest me?* Ten feet... *Will I lose my job if I'm arrested for assault and battery?* She has spotted me. Her pizza lies half eaten on her plate. Her hand covers her mouth and words are whispered to her sister. Five feet... They both stare at me. *Should I steal the pizza?* I am not a confrontational person, but I need to do something. What she did to me was not okay. Our eyes meet and lock. But something happens. I freeze. In the moment when I am in striking distance of my enemy, I pussy out. I keep walking, right past them, close enough to pull Sarah's hair, but I don't. I walk to the ATM on the other side of the food court, and pretend to extract money.

With my fake money, I slip out the back door of the mall and run to my car. I sit there for an hour, trying to digest what just happened. My hands are gripped tight on the steering wheel. Was I stupid? Did I just blow the only chance I ever had at saying just the right thing to the right person at the right time? What happened to my Machiavellian plan? The conditions were perfect. It was a public place. She would have been caught off-guard. It would have ruined her day, her week, and her month. Maybe she would have cried over her guilt. Even if she had sobbed 1/8th of the amount I have, it would have been worth it.

But there's something else happening. Like a newly-released prisoner, I'm starting to realize that for the first time in ten years there is no heavy burden sitting atop my shoulders. Life with Jack was a constant struggle. If it wasn't money problems, it was his drinking, his self-medicating, or his depression. I never knew what would be waiting on the other side of the door.

I exhausted myself trying to save him. I signed him up for school, after he insisted that was the one thing missing in his life. He never went. I handed money over to him constantly, after he convinced me that any of the following items would make his life worth living: a full sleeve of tattoos, two video games a week, a new computer, a motorized scooter, a motorcycle, and/or a new car. But nothing mattered. It was never enough for him. I was never enough for him.

Then, one day last year I found him passed out on the floor with fifteen or so of his prescribed tranquilizers missing from the bottle. When I couldn't wake him up, I called in my father. Together we brought him to, gave him water, sat him up and questioned him. *It was an accident*, he claimed, he *lost count*. The truth is he was trying to escape me. That day shook me to my core. I walked on eggshells around him for months, trying so hard to fix what was broken between us. When I finally figured out that it was me, that *I* must be causing his unhappiness, I tried to force him out. I wanted him to be happy, so I offered him leave. I helped him find an apartment, and even volunteered to pay the first month's rent. But in the end, he needed *me* more than he needed his freedom. And he hated himself for it.

I have to admit, I stayed with him for a long time because I was afraid of what would happen to him if I left. Would he swallow the whole bottle of pills next time? Would it be all my fault? He was never going to leave if Sarah hadn't come along. And in the end, I think that's what really prevented me from confronting her in the mall, and what caused me to finally abandon my revenge fantasy. The truth was, I was afraid to break them up. Somewhere deep inside of me, I was sad that he left, but even more terrified that he would want to come back, and that I would not have the fortitude to deny him. My heart finally caught up to what my brain already knew. I was over him.

Chapter Fourteen

Letting go of Jack once and for all means letting go of our life together and, more importantly, the home we shared. So the decision to move from Clarks Summit to Wilkes-Barre, where my job has been relocated, should be an easy one. But no decision is coming easy these days, everything is saturated in sentiment. My apartment in Clarks Summit that I shared with Jack is one of the only things left in my life that has remained the same. It became a home to me when I desperately needed one. It was the longest I had lived anywhere since I left my parents' house. But, the walls contain an echo of a life I'm working hard to forget, and it's starting to feel less and less like home. I am moving. Again.

I have decided to live in an old school house in an area that is on the edge of Wilkes-Barre's restoration project. It's a block away from where I work, and a million miles away from the memories I'm trying to outrun. The square three-story building was an elementary school in its former life, until it was abandoned by the city. Then, three years ago a developer from New York City bought her and turned her insides into twelve loft apartments. Her inhabitants were mostly college students, belonging to the university down the street. The rest were like the building itself, in transition, shedding their old skin for something new.

Maintenance men were painting plaster on the walls the day I was supposed to preview my new place. The building manager, Fay, a woman in her sixties, led my father and me through a maze of narrow hallways to the vacant living space. I would be living in the Principal's office. An irony not lost on my father.

"Now, I must warn you," Fay said with her shiny red nails on the brass doorknob, "they are finishing up some work inside."

The heavy steel door opened and a puff of heat and chalk dust came billowing out into the hallway. The sounds of saws and hand tools drowned out the classic rock playing from somewhere inside.

"Wow," my dad said and covered his mouth.

"Hmm, I guess they are not as far along as I had thought," said Fay.

"I'll take it," I shouted over the noise, despite not being able to see a thing.

I had lived with Jack since I was nineteen years old. Since my parents divorced and sold my childhood home. Now, I would be living somewhere alone. In a place that Jack will probably never see. It felt foreign to me, to be setting up house without him. I felt an enormous sense of sadness and relief all at once. I had craved a new start for so many years, but I was terrified of what that would mean. It was time. I had been living in that apartment surrounded by Jack and the memories of us as a couple for months now. I couldn't take it anymore.

Even though Jack had moved back to his mother's house, he had left almost everything he ever owned in our apartment (with the exception of his new electronics, of course). In the attic sat thirty boxes of old video games, countless old computers, and a dozen piles of computer books and manuals. In what used to be his office sat shelves of action figures, various electronic parts I could never identify, and some small furniture. I had called him a hundred times, had offered to box it all up for him, even put it on the porch so he would not have to enter our house. Yet, he still refused to come. He never even returned my calls. So I did what any rational person would do: the last weekend I spent in my old apartment, I rented a dumpster and began throwing everything away.

Soon, the reach of my purge expanded to items that Jack and I owned as a couple. Gifts I received at my shower, items that we used together, and anything else that smelled of the life we were supposed to live together. I wanted it gone. I wanted us gone. I wanted to forget that it ever happened, that I could marry someone and divorce someone all in the span of two years. I wanted to forget how stupid I was. I told myself it was a cleansing process, and it was. I was cleansing my life of a bad marriage, bad karma, and bad memories. Looking back on it, the idea to throw almost everything I owned into a dumpster may not have been the smartest thing I ever did, but I still maintain to this day that it was the most satisfying.

"You've gone crazy, Amye," my Grandmother cried over the phone when I told her what I was doing. My grandmother lived through The Depression; disposing of *anything* was equivalent to a mortal sin in her book. She has even been known to wash plastic grocery bags and hang them out on her clothesline to be reused.

"Gram, I'm actually thinking quite clearly." I huffed and puffed through my sentences as I struggled to lift boxes over my head.

"I called your cousin, Dawn. She's coming to look through your house before you throw anything else away."

"Better tell her to hurry," I said and hung up.

Twenty minutes later, my cousin, Dawn, and her latest boyfriend pulled into my driveway just as I began to hurl my artificial Christmas tree over the side of the dumpster.

"What are you doing?" Dawn yelled as she popped from the passenger side like a balloon with a leak.

"I'm throwing shit out! What does it look like?"

Mark, her boyfriend, approached with caution. I only met him once or twice before that day and he was clearly unsure as to how to react. I was running on pure adrenaline, which I imagine to him looked similar to being crazy.

"Amye, you need to chill out," Dawn warned.

"No, I'm cool, really. This is just the beginning of the purging process. I need to just start over, hit the reset button. I feel great, I swear." And I did. This was the best I felt in months. I had been living in a state of limbo. An illusion. The present shrouded in the past. Now, a decision had been made and I was *doing something* about my life instead of letting my life do things to me.

Mark ran over, his shoes slipping out from under him on the smooth dirt driveway. The last week had been filled with rain instead of snow, a typical northeast February thaw. The rain on Thursday continued into Friday and caused the dry dirt to bake into something resembling a dry mud. It was like running on chocolate cake icing. He pulled the Christmas tree from my arms and set it standing upright on the front stoop.

"You want it? It's yours," I said and headed back into the house for my next victim.

"What the hell is all of this?" Dawn asked.

I had put everything I wanted to throw out in plastic mail crates. I then organized them into rows, like a flea market. Dawn walked through the house and began pulling items that caught her eye.

"You're throwing away your mixer? This is a three hundred dollar mixer." She stood there in the middle of what looked like a million mail crates holding my cobalt blue Kitchenaid mixer, the one my mother surprised me with at my bridal shower.

"Take it," I answered and walked past her with a crate full of dishes. Moments later they exploded like a scatter bomb inside the green receptacle outside. It felt wonderful. Tears streamed down my face as each dish slapped and cracked against the metal. It was all of my bad energy going into that dumpster and bursting apart.

Pretty soon, Dawn could not keep up. Her boyfriend was outside still trying to get the Christmas tree in the back seat of their Chevy Malibu and I was practicing my fast ball with long stemmed wine glasses. I stood at the top of my front steps for a better angle, wound my arm up like a pitcher, and threw, hard. The glass shattered into a puff of chalky white dust.

"I'm taking this stuff," Dawn said emerging from the house carrying a crate loaded with my personal belongings.

"Go ahead, enjoy!"

They squeezed the tree into the car and loaded their newfound treasures into the trunk. Years later, I visited Dawn and Mark at Christmas only to find they had set up the tree exactly as I had for so many years before. And when I say exactly, I mean all of the ornaments remained the same as well, including the personalized pieces that read "Amye and Jack, First Christmas together, 2001."

Now, I am here and much lighter, in this new space without Jack. My father and I have spent the whole day moving my things into my new loft apartment. The ground outside has frozen again, and we must carefully navigate the patches of ice in the parking lot. Jennie and I have ended up moving on the same weekend. Jennie, my mother, and my mother's new husband, Joe, are two-hundred miles away unloading a truck in Brooklyn, New York. My mother and Joe have been together for about four years now, but only recently decided to get married. They got married in a Vegas drive-thru. Now, he was already helping one of us move. Welcome to the family.

"Amye, I want to talk to you," my father says after we finish. The sun has set and the only light we have is a small desk lamp. Every other light bulb was broken in the move. My father sits on the couch and pats the empty space next to him.

"What?" I say as I sit down, already defensive.

"Are you okay, kiddo?" the skin around his eyes pinches at the corners. We squint to see one another.

"I'm fine, why?"

"Are you drinking too much?" he asks and throws his left arm around my back.

Jennie. "No, Dad, why? Did Jennie say something?" Jennie had asked me that very question only days earlier, and it's never a coincidence when one of my parents ask right after. My father is worried about me. That's what he does. Having come from a family that never expressed their emotions, my father shows his through a series of safety checks.

When I was a teenager and sulking in my room over a boy, he would peek in and ask if I remembered to lock the car, or if I had enough money for lunch the next day. When he and my mother were divorcing and he knew I was taking it hard, he'd call me in my college apartment and ask if my smoke alarms needed batteries, or if I remembered to lock my door. Then, like a tightrope slacking at the edges, his voice would reveal the slightest sliver of emotion, and I would tumble into his warm and loving concern. Now, he is doing it again. I want to bitch about Jennie and her big mouth, but his sudden regard makes me soften. I'm so lucky to have parents who not only notice my self-destructive behavior, but care enough to try to stop it. I am so grateful for him.

"Dad, honestly. I am not drinking too much," I say and lean into his thick arm.

The truth is, I was never a drinker, never really touched a drop. But lately, it has helped to numb things a little.

"You know you can come to me about anything, right, Pumpkin?" my father reminds me as he gets up to leave. I want wrap my arms around his waist and beg him to stay. I want to tell him how I don't think anyone will ever really love me for who I am. How I don't feel like I belong anywhere, like I was misplaced and can't find my way back home. I want to sob and tell him that I am convinced I will never find true happiness. How I feel ugly and useless, and small, and that I wasted so much of my life on a man who didn't appreciate it. But I can't. The pain is like an avalanche inside of me, and I'm afraid he will be buried.

"I mean it, Aim, there isn't anything we can't figure out," he yells before closing the door.

You can't help me now, Dad, I think to myself. *No one can.*

Chapter Fifteen

Outside of my office sits a printer as big as a desk. It's the type of thing you'd see on *Saturday Night Live* as a spoof of what computers used to look like. It's a dot matrix antiquated machine that should be put out of its misery. Yet, everyday at 3:45pm, I stand with my hips pressing against the cream colored casing, watching what looks like a record player needle zip numbers back and forth across gray bar. Gray bar is a certain type of paper. It's lined with light grey stripes and is the only paper on which I can print tomorrow's program log. If we run out of gray bar, we're screwed. The whole place will collapse in on itself.

The official broadcast day starts at four o'clock in the morning. While you're sleeping, the world of broadcast television is flipping over. At about twenty minutes before the flip, the Master Control Operator pulls the next day's program log, writes his initials in the upper right hand corner, downloads the matching automation, and prepares for the transition. The Master Control Operator, Chris, is my opposite. He is the bizarro Traffic Manager. It is his job to deconstruct what it took hours for me to assemble. He is confined in a glass booth with a soft leather chair, three television monitors, a computer, and a board adorned with knobs and dials of every shape and size. When a commercial break happens, Chris must make sure what's on my program log matches what flashes on air.

Because we have such a technical job, and because everyone in my department is somewhat young, with the exception of my assistant manager, Billy, we have fun with the fact that we deal with logs all day. We have been known to utter uncomfortable sayings in a crowded elevator:

"Ugh, I can't wait to get my log out so I can go home."
"This log is really giving me trouble."
"My log was huge today!"

My traffic department consists of me, "the manager," Billy, my assistant manager and three assistant traffic coordinators. At twenty-five years my senior, Billy is the dad of our department. He hands out advice, he kills spiders, he jumps to my defense when I'm being reprimanded for a department error. He is a great assistant manager; he comes in early, stays late, knows everything there is to know about our printer (like how to fix it, which is required daily), and keeps to himself. In a department of five women, that's not an easy task. He is a loving father with three sons whose bright white smiles stick out from underneath baseball caps in photos taped all over his cubicle.

From the doorway of my office, I can see him in his cubicle with his salt and pepper head buried in gray bar paper, scribbling notes in the margins with a mechanical pencil, moving commercials away from competing products. Adequate separation, they call it. No local Ford dealership wants to see a Chevy commercial run in the same break as its own. And if that same Ford dealer pays for two spots during Judge Judy, one better run at the start of the show, and one better run at the end. Or they will come looking for a refund, forty-five dollars back in their pockets.

I've been in the new Wilkes-Barre building for only a few days when I wander into Master Control and meet Smithy. He's bald, carrying a spare tire around the middle, and has a nose that is ballooned in size thanks to two breaks in the mid-nineties. It's off-putting at first. This short, heavy teardrop shaped man sitting in the leather chair where my friend Chris was supposed to be.

"Hey, is Chris around?" I ask as I open the glass door.

"He's working downstairs now, I'm here," Smithy answers. This does not surprise me. Master Control Operators get paid shit money, and are responsible for a lot. This leads to high turnover. Every couple of months there is a new face behind the glass.

"Oh. Hi, my name is Amye," I say while tugging at my skirt. Wearing skirts to work is a new experience for me. Having lost fifty pounds now, I am halfway to my goal and feeling fantastic. Even though it's barely ten degrees outside, I'm stretching the boundaries of the professional dress code: tight T-shirts, short jean skirts, anything to show off what I have accomplished. Anything to help snare a man. My coworkers are looking the other way, but the whispers are accumulating around the perimeter. *What is she wearing? How much weight did she lose? Not that much…*

"Hi," he stands and outstretches his sweaty little paw, "I'm Jonathon, but you can call me Smithy."

"Oh, a nickname?"

"Sort of. I'm in a band and everyone just sort of calls me that."

"Oh, what band?" I am suddenly interested. It's like a dormant gene inside of me clicks on. My father was in bands his entire life, his father before him. I come from a line of local band boys and the women who loved them. I enter the glass room fully now, and rest my ass against the counter, making myself comfortable.

"I was in Breaking Benjamin, have you heard of them?" Smithy asks casually, knowing full well everyone has heard of them by now. Behind him three small monitors buzz with life. On one, Judge Judy is condescendingly asking a young girl if her parenting skills are what they should be. On another, the first commercial in the upcoming break sits frozen, poised and ready. It looks like a bank commercial, a man handing money over to a teller, their expressions not yet animated. On the third and final monitor, our local news crew can be seen getting ready for the five o'clock show. Smithy turns his back to me as he adjusts lighting levels and fiddles with sound knobs. But he keeps the very edge of his vision on my nicely toned legs.

"Wow! Really?" A million questions zip line through my mind. *Why are you working here*, comes out in front.

"Well, I was in Breaking Benjamin right as they got signed. Now I'm in a local band called Perfect Vision."

"That's impressive. I'll have to come and hear you guys play some night. Do you play around here?"

"Yeah, we do. Hey, I'll tell you what, have you ever heard of Afroman?" Smithy turns to look at me and I am suddenly taken by how blue his eyes are.

"The guy who sings that song about getting high?"

"Yeah, he's playing a small show tonight at Murray's. Would you want to go?"

I agree and spend the next hour convincing Georgia to leave her toddler son on a week night to spend three hours in a small bar listening to a songwriter whose skills only seem to shine when he's stoned. I tell her about Smithy, the paisley shaped boy who has caught my eye.

We are to meet at Murray's bar in Wilkes-Barre. One thing that sets Wilkes-Barre apart from Scranton is her downtown. While Scranton's downtown is a cluster of two-story buildings freckled by an occasional architectural marvel, Wilkes-Barre's epicenter is shaped by the Susquehanna River. The Susquehanna River is wide and strong, and throughout their history together, Wilkes-Barre has been both at her mercy and betrothed to her beauty. She winds in and around the city like a noose, tightening. In 1972, Hurricane Agnes ripped the river from her sleeping bed and submerged most of the city under water. Wilkes-Barre was ravished, buildings were almost completely destroyed. But the citizens did not give up, and in a monumental fiscal undertaking, the city restored almost all of its mansions and historical buildings.

Murray's Bar is a product of this restoration effort. When you walk through the front door, the twenty-foot ceilings catch your eye first, followed by the stone work that runs from floor to ceiling, then you get stuck on the stained glass windows and the mahogany bar. I spot Smithy and his friend in the far left corner sitting at a low lit table. This is it. I suck my stomach in as far as it goes, run my hands over my silky black hair, and begin my first unofficial, somewhat, kinda date.

The rest of my night with Smithy comes to me in flashes the next morning. I am alone, in my bed, with all of my clothes still intact. I have almost no memory of how I got here, and the little recollections I do have float into my mind like ashes from a cooling fire.

First there is Afroman, big and black with cherry eyes. Smithy and I are sitting at his table. The crowd is minimal. He smells like my college apartment after my roommate brought her bong back from home one weekend.

Then, between songs, there are shots. Three, six, nine, we order them by the round. Me, Smithy, and Afroman. Afroman speaks in a deep bass line, the notes curling my toes. He thinks I'm pretty, loves my breasts. Smithy does too; he chimes in from a safe distance. *This is what it's like to feel sexy*, I think to myself.

Later, Georgia is crying in the bathroom, mascara running rivers down her smooth tan face. Her mother is sick, hospitalized. They don't know what's wrong. Her pink cell phone shakes in her hands. *I can find my own way home*, I tell her. *Go, be with your mom.*

Then, Smithy and I are lumped together on the leather front seats of his car. Frost has formed on the windshield. I suck and lick his pale tree trunk of a neck. I tug at his clothes, trying to free him from their grasp. He pushes me away, hard. *Just friends*, he whispers.

And now, I'm here. In my bed, the far-away sunlight cracking through the windows, my mouth as dry as sand. The disaster of the night weighing me down, forbidding me to move from my bed. I pluck my cell phone from my pocket, call off work, pull the covers over my head, and go back to sleep. When I emerge from my cocoon of self pity hours later, Georgia is on the other end of my phone, crying.

"My mother has cancer," she sobs.

"What?!"

"It's bad, Aim."

"How bad?" I light a cigarette and the smoke swirls around me. I sink into my tan couch. Miscellaneous parts of my body are sore, the backs of my legs, my inner arms, my neck, there is no pattern to the pain.

"Stage four colon cancer," Georgia recites what the doctor told her. Apparently, stage four is as close to the final act as you're going to get without the curtain closing.

"I don't know what to say," I tell her, and for a moment there is a comfortable silence between us. Our breaths are synchronized through Cingular's satellites.

"Me either."

Chapter Sixteen

Dieting can turn you into a real bitch. Take any well-fed animal and deprive them of food for three days, then put any weaker creature in front of them and watch the carnage ensue. The same logic applies to the women of Weight Watchers. Take the sweetest, chubbiest little fat girl you can find in here, put her on a diet, and the same thing happens. Suddenly we become beasts, willing to engulf those who get between us and food. We are alcoholics without our drinks, drug addicts looking for our next fix, and when we don't get it, we can get ugly.

Oh sure, when you run into us at the doctor's office or the supermarket, we can be perfectly congenial. I might nod my head, touch your arm, and even pitch my voice in the perfect places as I *ooh* and *ahh* at the seventy-five million pounds you've shed this year "without even trying." But don't be fooled, not even for a minute. I wouldn't hesitate to grab a paring knife from the utensil aisle, gut you from stem to stern, and assume your metabolism.

It's this putrid, rotting evil inside of us that our fearless leader, Pantsuit Pam, knows so well.

"I hated my mother for so much of my life," she moans one Thursday night as we sit watching her every move. She is slumped in a silver chair in front of the room. Her knees shake, and her high-heeled sandals bump together every so often. *Nerves. She knows we can turn on her at any moment.*

"My mother was beautiful and thin, and never had to worry about putting on weight or dieting," she continues, "I loved her, yet I hated her so much. I always thought she had it so easy. I thought she could eat and drink whatever she wanted without a care in the world. Meanwhile, if I even touched a Twinkie I gained five pounds. Do any of you know someone like that? Someone who can eat anything they want?"

A tiny paw next to me flies into the air. This is a new girl. I've never seen her before. Yet, I know her so well. I can smell her a mile away. The determination brewing in her eyes, the welcome booklet brand new next to her thigh, a points calculator without even a crinkle. She is a blank slate on which Pam can work her magic. She is an outsider among us. She is dressed up, not yet privy to the insider rules, the language spoken between us sisters. She is Joanie from Minooka.

"Okay Joanie, let's hear it. Who do you know?" With a

sweeping hand motion, Pantsuit Pam encourages Joanie to stand.

"My brother," Joanie squeaks. "As we were growing up I *hated* him." She huffs and puffs the word hate through the air like she is blowing up a balloon.

"Why?"

"He was thin and never had to think about what he put in his mouth," Joanie responds.

"Are you sure about that Joanie?"

Joanie freezes. Her nostrils flare as she sheepishly looks to us for the answer. I cannot help but chuckle. It's a classic Pantsuit Pam curveball.

With another hand motion, Pantsuit Pam instructs Joanie to sit back down and begins writing something on the mobile, rolling chalkboard that faces all of us. Three words: THE BLAME GAME.

"It's easy to blame others for what is happening to us, isn't it? It's easy for us to direct our anger at the healthy people in our lives." Pantsuit Pam never uses the word "skinny" when describing a person; it's always the adjective "healthy." "I want all of you to think long and hard about that person you are directing all of your envy towards. Because that's what it really is, isn't it? Jealousy? Envy? Think about what they eat, what they put into their mouths. Is it really *anything* they want?"

I don't have to think long and hard about where I have always directed my unwarranted rage. My anger has always been pointed precisely at Jennie. In my mind, having a thin sister was the cruelest joke of all. It was the universe's way of saying "fuck you." Jennie was perfect. She was thin, beautiful, and smart, without even trying. She fluctuated between a size two and a size zero for most of her life. She never really cared for junk food, tended to turn down a piece of cake (which I gladly accepted on her behalf), and was never really one to be taken in by the golden arches.

I remember lying on Jennie's bed as a teenager, with one elbow holding my head as I watched her ready herself for a night out. In the mirror, she would bite her bottom lip as she spread blue eyeliner across her lids with the precision of a surgeon. Together, we would cough in the cloud of hair spray used to coif her high bangs. When it came time to pick out clothes, there was no camouflaging, no crying, no sucking anything in or trying to conceal bulging rolls. Everything was easy. Simple. Clothes just slipped over her, like a block of ice gliding across a smooth floor.

I remember going to restaurants with her and watching in amazement as she glossed over the burger menu and ordered a salad or a grilled chicken breast. I would think to myself, *what is wrong with you?* If I was that skinny, I would eat junk food all day. I would eat fast food for every meal, down chocolates like they were breath mints, and take baths in hot fudge. I would bleed milkshakes.

Now, fifteen long years later, as my car winds a particular curve that signals home, a light bulb blinks on in my brain. Jennie could not eat anything she ever wanted because she was skinny. Jennie was skinny *because* she didn't eat anything she wanted. She made smart choices and only ate until she was full. She passed on cake when she could, and never felt the need to lick her plate clean. She had a healthy relationship with food. Something I have never had.

As I pull into the driveway that chokes my apartment building like a moat of broken pavement and neglectful maintenance, I turn off my car's engine and begin to cry. Pieces are falling into place inside of me. Sparks are igniting, synapses are connecting, and the bigger picture is starting to come into focus. No one else is to blame for my weight problem. The universe is not giving me a big fuck you. It's me. It's all me. It's my fault.

Chapter Seventeen

Mine was never a love story. It was an obligation story. I was with Jack because my parents were splitting up, selling the house, and I had nowhere else to live. I was with Jack because he needed to escape his horribly dysfunctional family. I was with Jack because we bought a car together and if I wasn't there, he would never pay for it. I was with Jack because I was fat and no one else would love me. I was with Jack because I wanted babies and even if a miracle happened and I did find one more man on this earth to love me, I just didn't feel like starting all over again with someone else. And Jack was with me because he loved me.

This is the latest mind fuck that has my stomach in a knot. I'm lying in bed, staring at my low, concrete ceiling, and listening to the woman upstairs walk back and forth in what must be twenty-inch heels. Click, click, click. Click, click, click. I have deduced, through tracking her movements, that her kitchen must be directly overhead. And that she makes breakfast at around 6:15 every morning. *Click, click, click*, it's my alarm.

Even though we are only weeks from our divorce becoming final, Jack and I are still throwing occasional punches at one another. Our latest blowout happened via email. Delivered around noon, my stomach seized at the sight of the blue mail icon with his last name attached. A last name that, until next month, is still attached to me. The problem is the car. The car he wanted, and now has, but will not pay for. The bank behind the car is calling me daily. Threatening to sue us, to repossess the car, to prevent me from ever borrowing another penny, to burn down my house, to kill my grandmother.

But, the truth is, aside from wanting my grandmother to remain alive, I couldn't care less about their threats. It's become a stance of principle. *If you've ever loved me, you'll pay the car loan. You live at home with Mommy for free, I'm supporting myself in an apartment, you have it better than I do. You have the car, I don't. Pay the fucking car payment.* It's a measuring stick of his love. But Jack is smart and resorts to guerilla warfare. In the middle of an argument, he plants a land mine deep inside of my brain. *I loved you, and never stopped. You just could not accept my disease. You were selfish.* This bomb lies dormant for hours. Then, in the middle of a dead sleep, it ignites and explodes, leaving guilt everywhere in its wake. I jump awake with tears streaming down my face. Is he right? Did I abandon him? If only I had stopped expecting so much from him, would we have had a better marriage, a happier marriage?

Jennie is half asleep in a Brooklyn brownstone two hundred miles away from me, when I ring her awake one morning with my sobs.

"Are you serious?" her husky voice cracks.

"Yes. I feel like this guilt is going to eat a hole through me."

"Amye. You have nothing to feel guilty about. We've been through this."

And we have, a million and one times since Jack and I broke up. But this nagging worry is like a parasite, eating my confidence and sanity. I've read Jack's accusatory emails over and over. *You said awful things to me. You abused me. You were a monster.* And despite Jennie's rational explanations, her morning, afternoon, and nightly phone calls where we spend hours poring over every detail, every moment of wrongdoing on my part, I still can't quiet that voice that whispers: *What if he's right? What if I am to blame for everything?*

This guilt is familiar and warm. It's been with me since the beginning. It's kept me from moving on, from kicking Jack out, and from losing weight. It's been an anchor holding me from happiness. If I left Jack, in my heart or in my mind, the guilt was there, stuffing me back into that box from which I was trying desperately to escape.

"Amye, the relationship was toxic. It wasn't good for either of you." Jennie continues her line of reasoning. My sister's so good to me, willing to hold her phone cocked in the crook of her neck while she bats her eyelashes under a thick mascara brush. Putting me on speaker while an electric razor zips around her bony legs. It's times like this that I feel so badly for ever having resented her for being skinny. She has been my rock through all of this, and I suddenly don't give a shit what size she is.

"The only thing you're guilty of is staying too long. You should have left his ass years ago," Jennie says over the swooshing of her hairspray.

"I know. I know."

The truth is, I had plenty of chances to escape. There had been other women before Sarah, other indiscretions on his part. First there was Tracy, a girl from his past who popped up like an ugly rash in the middle of our relationship. We had been dating only months, when, on a camping trip, Jack announced he was seeing her and, thus, leaving me. It took a few weeks, but he eventually came calling, sliding back into my open and waiting arms.

The second time, we were married. Solidified as husband and wife for nine months. Her name was Jamie and she was an employee under Jack at a video game store in the Steamtown Mall. He had come home one Friday night and confessed that he had kissed her, felt her up, let his hands drift to her breasts, his tongue dabble in her mouth. I was horrified, heartbroken, and really, really angry.

I would like to say that I took the news with dignity. That I uncrossed my legs, stood up, walked to the bedroom, packed my things, and left. But I was young and hot tempered. I was insecure and defensive. I was fat and lonely and scared of losing the one man that claimed to love me. So we fought. Like we always did: ugly and violent.

The next day, Jack took back his words, claimed he had made a mistake, and that he was staying with me, staying home. I didn't leave then, because Jack convinced me that I had driven him to it. I was too hard on him, always pressuring him to be something he could never be: a man, responsible, social, considerate… I begged and pleaded, screamed and yelled, and acted like a raging lunatic sometimes. I was Sisyphus, and Jack was my boulder. I was forever pushing him, and getting nowhere.

But there was always that one, tiny thought in the back of my mind. Was I a monster? What kind of person hits and screams and throws anything within her reach? Was I already a psychotic raging freak at twenty years old? Were those women just Jack's way of trying to escape from me? These are the questions I pose to Jennie, every time we talk. Over and over again. There is a cauldron of boiling uncertainty inside of me, threatening to burn me to the ground.

"No," she yells over the buzzing traffic finding its way into her Bluetooth. Her teeth chatter between sentences from the winter air. There are laws against blowing your horn on certain streets in New York City, but no one really obeys. It's called noise pollution. After a while, the honking, the sirens, the cursing and yelling becomes white noise to your life, to our phone calls, to Jennie's reasonable reassurance of my state of mind. "You are not crazy!" she yells.

"I hit him once, after I found out he cheated," I confess. It's almost nine o'clock now, I should have been at work twenty-five minutes ago. Tears stream down the sides of my cheeks.

"What do you mean you hit him?" Jennie is breathless as she runs across a crowded street on her way to work.

"I hit him," I repeat.

"So what?" she says. "I would have fucking killed him."

Chapter Eighteen

Back at work, Smithy reminds me over and over that he will never have me as a girlfriend. He will never be the answer to my problems. But that doesn't stop me from trying. I spend weeks trying to lure him into commitment. I have sex with him whenever he wants, I follow him from stage to stage across two cities, and I am a good friend to him. Better than he is to me. For all of his faults, however, Smithy is never dishonest with me. He reminds me again and again that he is cemented in his life as a local musician and can never be the boyfriend I'm looking for. But I still don't get it. I keep trying and trying. And then, one night, it happens. Like a curtain called to the rafters, I suddenly see what has been in front of me the whole time.

It's a cold night in March and I'm throwing an informal get together. A few people from work have come over to have a few drinks. I'm so close, they can walk to my apartment. My friend, Joe, lives just down the street and has made a habit of planting himself on my couch with his feet lifted onto the coffee table. Smithy and I are deep in conversation in the kitchen when Joe calls us over.

"Um, guys? Look who is on the television," Joe says, motioning towards the TV screen.

Smithy walks over to the television and his face freezes. There in front of us is Jay Leno welcoming the band Smithy left behind. The lead singer looks like an old friend as he and Leno chat about their new album, their tour, and the band's small town roots. Smithy's stare has changed. The blood has now returned to his face, and in a flush of emotion, his eyes begin to well up. Joe and I exchange glances of desperation.

"I'll get us another beer," Joe says, "Smithy, you want another?"

"Yeah, please," Smithy answers.

"Are you okay?" I ask as the band starts to play a song for Jay Leno and half of America.

"I helped write that album you know, the first one? Now he won't even take my calls," Smithy's voice trails off as he talks.

"We'll I'm sure there is a reason why this all happened," I lie.

"Yeah, they're rich, and I'm not."

I sit in silence. Smithy looks at me for some sort of condolence, but I have nothing. What would I say? That even though the odds of a local band selling platinum albums are astronomically low, it could, possibly, happen again? That he would be the only person on earth to receive two offers to become famous? He blew it. He knows it, and so do I. We sit there for another twenty minutes, pretending what just happened on the *Tonight Show* didn't. Soon, the night ends as it usually does: I have too much to drink, Joe goes home, and Smithy gets lucky.

"Will you do something for me?" I ask, after we have sex. The apartment is quiet and dark. My head is on his chest, listening to the inner workings of his body. The heartbeat, the lungs pushing breath from his mouth. I close my eyes and take in his smell.

"Will you stay with me tonight?" I blurt out. I hate this. I hate this side of me. The side of me that is paralyzed with the fear of spending one more night in this bed by myself. In my mind, our final roadblock, my divorce, is cleared. *He can fall in love with me now.*

"I can't, I have to get home, I have some shit to do," Smithy says, hopping out of bed and into his clothes.

"Like what?" I ask, I can see the outline of him from the streetlight outside. He is hurried.

"I have to take my mom to the doctors very early, I need to get home and sleep."

"Oh, okay, well I will see you at work tomorrow?" I ask.

"Of course, beautiful!" He smiles, and leans down to kiss my forehead. Sensing my disappointment, he adds "Hey, listen, we'll grab dinner tomorrow okay? I'll buy."

I hear the door close without the lock clicking. I waste no time throwing on my robe and running over to the oversized windows of my apartment. I know from experience it takes him about a minute and a half to go down the corridor of my building, out the back door, and through the parking lot to where I can see him getting into his car from my window.

In the building next to me, a party is brewing, a bunch of local college kids. I stay hovered in the window with the lights off behind me. I watch from the left hand corner, hiding myself, in case he turns around to pick a leaf off his shoe, or to investigate a noise, and spies me watching him. Soon Smithy appears and I watch as he pulls his keys from his pocket.

Suddenly, I see a girl from the building next door waving her arms to get his attention. Through the closed window I can hear a muffled yell of what I think is his name. He spins around and smiles as she runs towards him. She has a beer in one hand and hugs

98

Smithy with the other. They talk for a few moments. Then, with me watching, they walk happily into the building next door. I sit and wait for almost an hour before I decide to cry myself to sleep. When I leave for work the next morning, his car is in the same exact spot.

Two weeks later, Smithy informs me that he has decided to commit to a girlfriend. Only one problem: It's not me. She's a thick, red-haired girl who jiggles just like I did, right at the edge of his stage. But she's young, and the stars in her eyes are not temporary.

Years later, when the desperation has gone completely from my eyes, Smithy will tell me that his refusal to commit to me was for my own good, that he knew he would never be the type of boy who could lie in the grass on a warm day and read Yeats with me, that the cold concrete of a sticky barroom floor would always be his home. *You were too good for me, too smart, too normal.* I believe him, but a part of me can't help but love him just the same. He gave me the gift of music at a time in my life when I could only hear the noise.

Chapter Nineteen

Like any subculture, there is a dark side to being metabolically challenged. A seedy, bloated underbelly of the fat girl's world. It is the notion that we will do anything, and I mean *anything*, to get rid of the weight. But unlike drug cartels or the child sex slave industry, our underbelly runs without anyone getting rich. There is no exchange of cash, weapons, or virgins, just germs, lots and lots of germs. You see, it's not uncommon for fat girls to seriously consider catching diseases. Strep Throat, the Flu, sinus infections, all of them were once as welcomed at my house as my friends and family. Some may have mistaken this for sensitivity in the past, "Oh, Amye, she's so sweet. Willing to host Christmas Eve dinner even though all of us have stomach viruses." But make no mistake about it, you would be doing me the favor. And as I was licking your forks and glasses after you left, I'd be wishing and praying that you left something more than just your poorly chosen gift behind.

For me, the disease option morphed into reality when I was fourteen years old, and–after catching Mono from a boy at a party– I lost forty pounds in two months. For six weeks after the mono left my immune system ravaged and my spleen enlarged, I was stunning. I wore halter tops and frayed jean shorts. I strutted the streets like Julia Roberts in *Pretty Woman* (before she gets the red dress). I had no trouble meeting boys, and I collected scraps of paper with phone numbers on them as easily as catching snowflakes on my tongue. In school I was looked at with desire and not pity. It was the greatest two months of my life. Then, like an echo, the lost pounds returned home to their origin, and brought ten more with them.

But I never forgot that it was mononucleosis, a disease dreaded by most, that had aided me in my desperation to lose weight. It was mono that made me feel sexy, mono that made me remember what it was like to feel wanted and to be accepted among my peers. And from then on, diseases were the new trick, the latest fad, for getting a good jumpstart on a diet. I looked for them, I prayed for them, I even tried to create them by going outside with a wet head or eating cheese with a spot of mold. I once had a near run in with lesbianism just to catch a stomach flu that had helped a coworker of Georgia's lose ten plus pounds in only three days.

I know what you're thinking. There is an easier solution, a medicinally manufactured miracle that could make all of this go away. A pill, two pills, adrenaline, speed, a rush of something through my body that will make me less hungry and more active. But I have been lucky enough to have been scared off of diet pills. As a teenager working at Sears, I watched my plump coworker waste away in front of my eyes. It had been happening for months, the anorexia, the pills, the starvation, but none of us self-absorbed teenagers noticed. Then, when we finally did, she was a ghost; gaunt and hollow. Her ribcage rippled against her skin like an accordion, and her eyes were slowly being sucked backwards in to her skull.

One Saturday night she collapsed at work and when I saw her mother, days later, I was told the young woman had thrown her body into early menopause and would never be able to birth a child. She was thirty-one. It was enough to scare me away from pharmaceuticals for life.

The women at Weight Watchers keep all of this ugliness hidden from Pam. In the hallway before she and Joan, the shaky receptionist, open the doors to the meeting room there are usually ribbons of conversations floating through the air. Talk about how the week had gone, who struggled and who didn't. Idle chatter about stagnant gym memberships, snack-sized Kit-Kat bars, and stubborn scales. But if you listen close enough, put your ear into the wind and listen, you will hear the hum of something darker. Ribbons laced with bulimia, starvation, and self-loathing so deep the bottom could pop out at any second. Strings of pain, fear, absolute anguish. Whispers, really. Hushed stories of scabies, rabies, chicken pox, shingles, measles, hepatitis, and the golden calf: a parasite. Then, the door opens, the swoosh of the thin hollow wood and the chatter stops dead. Like parents who don't want to believe their teenagers are having sex, we are pretty sure Pantsuit Pam could never imagine what we are capable of.

As much as I would love a good flu right now, I'm not at that point, *yet*. For months now, the scale sliding to the left has come easy. Like two scissored blades gliding across an ice-covered pond. Sixty-five pounds have slipped from me like autumn leaves from their trees. The heavy weight, the brushed silver chunk of steel slides and slides and slides, further and faster towards thin. Then, one day it doesn't. For three weeks the scale betrays me. I gain one pound, then three, then two more, it's like a balloon is inside of me inflating a little more each week. I'm beginning to panic. To consider an option so pathetic, most of us will not even say it out loud. I'm starting to pay extra close attention to shopping cart handles and public bathrooms.

"It's called a plateau," Pantsuit Pam says after a meeting one night. The word drips from her lips like blood from a pinpricked finger. *Plateau.* I have stayed behind for a private consultation. Pam sits on the edge of the folding table at the back of the room like a Buddha resting on the cheap green tablecloth. Next to her a warm coffee pot sits half full.

"It's very common," she explains, "You've lost so much that your body is starting to acclimate itself to your current diet. What sorts of things have you been eating?" She fiddles with a stirrer in her Styrofoam cup. A half moon of peach lipstick is stamped on one side.

"I don't know," I stammer, "I'm not sure."

Pantsuit Pam twists her lips like a pretzel, and for a minute I feel like she is staring right through me. Right through my bullshit. Like she has a kaleidoscope to the past and can see me stuffing my face with pretzels and wine and not much else.

"Are you drinking the water?" she asks.

The water. The required sixty-four ounces daily. It's their answer to everything. Not losing weight? Drink the water. Feeling lethargic? Drink the water. Pregnant with your husband's best friend's baby? Drink the water! Diagnosed with stage four lymphoma? Drink the water! It's as if we were all born with a water deficiency that if remedied, will morph us all into supermodels.

"Yes. I drink tons of water," I say.

"Hmmm, maybe you're drinking too much water?"

"The water is not the problem," I snap. Pam and I are not entirely alone, a dark-haired, rather tall woman has lingered behind fiddling with something in her purse. She chuckles ever so quietly as Pam and I go back and forth.

"Listen, bring your food journal in next week. We'll look through it together," Pam assures me.

Afterwards in the hallway, the tall dark-haired woman waits for me. She greets me with a smile. "I couldn't help but overhear," she says. She is really quite pretty. She has thick brown hair that rests somewhere in the middle of her back. She has curves, nice ones, but not too many. They're actual curves and not rolls of fat molded into what could be mistaken for curves. She only has maybe twenty, twenty-five pounds to lose. She is beautiful, and as I do with every pretty woman, I immediately wish I could be her. I imagine wearing her clothes, her face, her life. I imagine what I would do with her body, the one she is clearly wasting. We chit chat for about five minutes as we walk to our cars, our feet clomping the ground in unison, and then it happens. As the sky darkens around us, her voice lowers and she whispers, barely audible... *You know, I once knew a woman who had scurvy. She couldn't hold her baby for three months, but then, she put on her clothes and they fell right off. A skirt, boom, right to the floor. She dropped like fifty pounds.*

For a moment, as I stand there staring into her dark eyes, I contemplate asking her about the woman. How did she catch it? Was it painful? Was it worth it? Then I imagine that skirt, hanging low from her hips like a ring of clouds sagging in the sky. But tonight something is different. As I stand in that parking lot and the street lights click on, I am at a crossroads. It's as if Pantsuit Pam is on one shoulder with her sixty-four ounces of water and her food journals, and this woman and her scurvy-ridden friend are on the other. I have a choice to make. I can repeat the same patterns I always have: looking for the easy way out, acting out of desperation and fear, and going down that forbidden road inside of myself where even Scurvy isn't off limits, or I can work the program, drink the water, and listen to the one woman who hasn't failed me yet.

"I'm sorry about your friend," I say as I turn to walk to my car with my keys jingling in my hand. "I hope she feels better." It isn't an easy decision, but it's one I have to make. I have changed everything about my life on the outside, now the remodeling has to extend to the internal. It may be dark in this parking lot, but inside of me a flame is beginning to flicker.

The following week I write down everything I put in my mouth. By the time the week is up, I break down in tears when I look at my list. I am embarrassed, ashamed, and resigned to the fact that I must face reality. It's a list full of beer and pretzels, sometimes soup or a can of green beans if I'm lucky. The Weight Watcher's program, when worked properly, consists of a balanced diet, healthy eating, and making tough choices. I have been succeeding in terms of losing the pounds, but have been failing miserably at the rest. I have not been eating healthy at all. I've been drinking too much. I have been crying too much. I have been lying too much. If I want to be thin, I have to work for it. I have to work hard and earn this reward. I must choose to go after what I want and do it.

I've lost over sixty pounds since I started Weight Watchers. But almost none of that has been a conscious decision. The progress I've made has been a knee-jerk reaction to a break up. My weight loss has been about getting back at Jack, or making Smithy love me. It's always been about something else, *someone else*. But now, my body is revolting against me, demanding that I change something. It is time to make my life and my choices about *me*.

At the next meeting I avoid Pantsuit Pam, and she seems to have forgotten our little pow-wow. I hide in the back of the room against the table with the coffee and its accoutrements, which include Splenda, Sweet and Lo, Equal, and fat free cream. No real sugar in sight. No doughnuts and icing-topped cinnamon buns like you'd find at any other group meeting. We can't be trusted in that way. At the front of the room Pam talks about listening to our bodies and hearing what they are saying. I imagine my body begging for mercy. *I've had enough McDonalds to last a fucking lifetime. Oh, and the beer is getting old too. And I don't think I can bounce back from Scurvy, so don't even think about it. Grow the fuck up. Stop treating me like I'm a dumpster in an alley somewhere.*

"Imagine. You are in complete control of your future," Pam says as she spins a chair around and straddles the cold aluminum. "What do you want for your life? What do you want your life to be?"

"I want my life to be about me for once," I blurt out. I almost don't recognize the words as they float from my throat out into the stale air of the room. The women turn to find where the unfamiliar voice has sprung from. My face flushes red, not from embarrassment as it always had before, but from the new fire smoldering in my belly.

"Then get to work," Pam says smiling.

Chapter Twenty

Before I can get to work on my new life, I get one last kick in the nuts from my old one. My grandmother is the first to call. It's early on a Sunday morning. The sun has just broken through the clouds and sneaks through my oversized windows like a Peeping Tom. I'm lying in the cavern of my white down-filled comforter when she breaks the news. There in the *Scranton Times* is my divorce decree, final and complete. I am officially single. I hang up the phone and drop back onto my pillow. *That's it. It's over.*

I remembered the day I filed for divorce, drove the papers down to Jack's house, held his hand while he signed them in front of me. My lawyer had offered to mail them, *he'll get a certified letter*, she promised, *it will all be tracked.*

I don't think you know who we are dealing with, I told her. The papers would be delivered but then would sit on a stack in his room for two months, a year, however long it took him to muster enough initiative to actually sign them and mail them back.

Not leaving anything to chance, I drove to his house, parked in the same spot I had parked in for the ten years I had been visiting his parents' house, knocked on the door I had once just winged open with familiarity, and marched upstairs to Jack's bedroom. He was drunk. It was a Saturday afternoon, around three or so, and I could spot his inebriation immediately. The smell of that red wine he always drank was like a rotten perfume, reminding me of the sourness between us. He looked wild-eyed, surprised to see me. He

105

stashed the half-empty gallon under the bed where it clinked and clanked against other empties. It went as it usually did.

Me: Sign these. (do something)

Jack: No. (do nothing)

Me: Please?

Jack: No.

Then came the weakness, the crying. The "let's run away together, Amye, where no one knows us and start over." Followed by the mantra: *Sarah doesn't know me. She's pressuring me to do things. She's not you. She's not you.* But I was never tempted. I realized that it didn't matter if anyone else knew us, because we knew each other and that was enough. "We don't like each other," I reminded him, and there wasn't a place in the world we could hide from ourselves.

When I drove away from him that day, I knew I was never going back. His parents' house, that bedroom, that bed, had been home to me for so many years. It felt weird to leave it all behind with no gush of pain or panic in my gut.

Jack and I had been through so much together. I had fallen apart, and he had put me back together more times than I care to remember. I can still feel his hands on my face or his whisper in my ear when he comforted me. We shared moments in that bedroom, in our life that would be only ours forever. When my parents divorced, one of the things that I always struggled to understand was how two people could build a life together, moment by moment, and then break it all apart and walk away. But with my signed divorce papers on the seat next to me as I drove away from Jack's that day, an understanding took root in my brain. What Jack and I shared was over. Things end. My family is drenched in failed marriages; even my great-grandparents were divorced. Things end and begin again, and people survive these breaks. And now, I was determined to be one of them: a survivor.

Chapter Twenty-One

To celebrate or commiserate my divorce, Georgia takes me to The Water's Edge Bar and Grill in Wilkes-Barre. It isn't long before I am sloppy-drunk on wine and leaning against the bar for physical support. Georgia stands next to me, her exposed back facing the crowd behind us. Her mother has been in and out of the hospital as the doctors try to extend her stay in this world. Georgia calls me late at night sometimes when her husband and son have gone to sleep, and I listen as she cries, her soft sobs like a whimper of abandonment.

"To your official divorce. To freedom," Georgia says and clinks her sweaty Miller Lite bottle (2 points) with my half-empty wine glass (2 points). She is happy here with me. She temporarily forgets the commitments pulling her home.

"Yeah, whoopee," I say back.

The bar is packed. It's one of the only places within five miles that doesn't card, so it draws a lot of very young looking twenty-one year olds. I am facing the bar in a high-back leather stool when I spot a gaggle of giggling girls squeeze through the glass double doors like a bubble bursting.

"Oh, look at this shit," I mutter and motion for Georgia to look at the girls who have begun dancing in place, mimicking strippers.

"Oh Jesus Christ," Georgia answers.

The girls are segregated in a corner of the bar, with three or four tables shoved together to make one. They bounce around in their tight tops and frosted hair. Everything looks ordinary until one of them climbs with her high heels onto the smooth, unbalanced tabletop. She wears a shirt that proudly proclaims: Kiss me, I'm the Bride to be!

Suddenly, all I want to do is save this young woman from a life of heartache. "I'm going to say something," I announce and slug back the rest of my pale red wine.

"No, Amye. You're not," Georgia warns me.

But before she can stop me, before she can put her short arms around me and prevent movement, the bartender asks her is she'd like a refill, and when she turns around I am gone like bad news shot across the dance floor.

"Hey!" I yell to the bachelorette now dancing at the bequest of a few men who have managed to wander over into her orbit. Her dark brown curls bounce long and lazy in front of her perfectly-powdered face.

"Can I help you?" A short friend steps in my path.

"No, I'm talking to your friend," I mumble and push past. "Hey!" I yell again.

The girl stops dancing, but her smile is still drunk and loose. She climbs down from the table, tipping the top behind her.

"Hi," she says and sips the dark cherry liquid through a straw from the glass in her thin, pale hand. Her face is even more delicate up close. A landscape of smooth, untouched snow. Her name is Brenda. Beautiful, young, untainted Brenda. I have to help her. It's my humanitarian reflex.

"You're getting married?" I ask.

"Yes."

"How old are you Brenda?"

"Twenty-two," she squeaks back. Her friends notice our conversation and start to migrate towards us. Suddenly we are in a huddle in the corner of the bar. The band has taken to the stage again and a song belonging to Pearl Jam moans from the speakers.

"What the fuck are you doing getting married so young?" My question blows through the huddle like a scatter shot. Suddenly the welcoming banter has ceased and their defenses go up. Brenda's face morphs into a muddle of confusion and anger.

"What?" Her voice is thin and small now.

"I said, what the fuck are you doing with your life? Getting married at twenty-two, are you goddamn crazy?"

"I...I...I, who are you?" Brenda looks at me for any sign of recognition. She comes up empty, but I do not. I recognize her. She is me. Making the same foolish mistakes, trusting people she shouldn't, giving up this tightly knit over-protective gaggle of girls for the love of a man who is fleeting at best. I want to save her, to climb inside of her and make the necessary adjustments to help her avoid the pain that will inevitably come her way.

"I am you in seven years, a hot mess," I answer.

"You don't know anything about her. How dare you say anything, Bitch," A strong voice chimes in from the huddle around us.

"Listen to me!" The seven glasses of wine I had earlier are starting to hinder my ability to make a convincing argument. My words and thoughts tangle like knots in my throat. "You're too young!"

"Listen you fat bitch, get the fuck out of here before I kick your ass." *There it is again, fat bitch. I'm still someone's fat bitch.* The small girl, the one who previously tossed herself between Brenda and me, is back. She's ready to fight. I look for Georgia, for her assistance in the form of brute strength, but she is stranded outside of this circle. Her head bobs in the distance and her mouth moves, yelling my name.

"I don't want any trouble. I just want her to think about what she is doing," I say. "Do you know how badly I wish someone had warned me?" My defense goes unheard and soon the short girl is shoving my shoulders with the palms of her thick little paws.

Brenda turns and walks away. I shrug off my short aggressor and start to follow her. But before I do, I feel two gigantic hands on my shoulders. A man's voice is dense, his grasp powerful. Before I can plead my case, I am asked to leave the bar. As I am escorted to the door, Brenda's curls fade from my view.

Outside, a group of young boys have gathered in the early spring air to smoke cigarettes. I wander over to them, pull the crushed and crinkled Newport box from my tight jean pockets, and ask for a light. Georgia rings my phone two or three times before I realize it's vibrating against my numb thighs. *I'm outside with some young, cute boys*, I tell her loudly. She sighs loudly and tells me to stay put. The boys enjoy my drunken stammering. They like how I sway back and forth on my chunky heels, like the hurricane-proof shopping mall they built in downtown Scranton a few years back. I sway with the wind, with the cold, to the music in my head. I lean against one boy, then another, then the building, and finally, I slide to the cold, still-frozen ground until one of the boys is kind enough to pull me to my feet and hand me over to a rather annoyed Georgia. In the car, the crying starts. The loneliness. I miss Jack, I miss my home. I don't know how to stop hurting. I don't know what to do with myself.

Georgia, not really sure how to make it better, drops me off at my father's house. Once there, he and I find ourselves on his back porch swinging slightly on a wooden rocker under a sky of blackness.

"I'm a disaster," I utter as tears stream down my face, "I feel so lost, Dad. I don't know where I belong."

"You're never lost, honey. You have me," he answers.

"But I have no home," I sob harder.

His arm around me is welcomed and warm.

"You're not a little girl anymore, honey. You have to make your *own* home now."

After another hour of my sobbing, my father will allow me to stay the night. He and his new wife, Doreen, will tuck me into their womb of a guest bed. My father will sit on the edge of the down comforter for what feels like hours, stroking my head as I cry into the puffy, white pillow. *It's okay, my girl. Everything is alright with the world.* I sleep like a baby, for the first time in months.

Chapter Twenty-Two

The next morning, my father's words are still seeping slowly through my soggy brain. *You have to make your own home.* Throughout

110

my entire life, my home has been something external. My parents' home, Jack's home, and finally, my home with Jack. It never occurred to me that my home could exist in the center of *me*, or that it could exist without the presence of someone else. That switch was never flipped on in my head because I had never been alone before in my life. I went from living with my parents right into a ten-year relationship. I had never come home to an empty house night after night and been expected to fill the space for myself. I never imagined what my own home would look like, who it would contain, or what would be inside. I'd never been in charge of my life the way I had the potential to now.

My father is right, as always. I have to start creating something *for* myself and *by* myself. A home. A life. I'm a grown woman, and I'm acting like a fucking idiot. It's time to pull my shit together and find my place in the world. I'm getting tired of living like this. I'm so engrossed in thought I don't hear the door open.

"Can I make you some breakfast?" my stepmother, Doreen, whispers. The sun is low and warm, across her face.

"What time is it?" I ask.

"It's almost eleven."

"I'll be right there," I say.

I cannot drag myself out of bed. My body is tired, my bones ache, my head feels like a bowling ball rolling in the canyon of a down-filled pillow. Yet, somehow this is the most at peace I have felt in months. The urgency which has fueled me for months seems to have dissipated in the nest of my father's house. There's something no one tells you about divorce: no matter how old you are, you can be seventy-five or twenty-five, it makes you feel *old*. You can almost hear this clock ticking in your eardrums, and your heart races as you try to keep up with everyone else in your generation.

When my marriage first ended, I thought: I'm twenty-eight, I have no kids, no house, nothing to show for my life. I have to start from square one. I have to meet someone, have a courtship, fall in love, get engaged, plan the whole wedding again (which is two years, easy), then, *maybe* try again to have kids. By the time that all happens, I could be forty years old. It felt impossible. Like I had some great chance to get it right the first time and I blew it. Now I would just have to keep running to catch up.

But today something is different. I'm sick to death of running. I'm not going to worry about keeping up. I'm going to listen to my body. I'm going to treat her well. I'm going to accept my life for what it is: full of family and friends. I'm going to work on getting a new job, something I love, rather than a job I simply tolerate. I'm going to start writing again, maybe go back to school. I don't need a man to feel complete. I will carve out a life for myself. I will pull myself out of this hole I've been dwelling in. It's like the gash left from my divorce is starting to heal, and it's time to remove the bandage.

At the breakfast table, my father reads his paper while Doreen fills our plates. He reads aloud the latest news from the war in Iraq, adding colorful commentary along the way. Meanwhile, I calculate an eight-point breakfast. Two points for each egg, and three points for bacon. It's the most nutritious breakfast I've eaten in a year. My father's house is warm and bright. His small dog runs over and collapses on my bare feet. This simple act, sitting at a breakfast table eating with people who love me, feels good. It fills my chest with a warmth I have been missing.

"Amye, why don't you stay the weekend?" Doreen asks as she sits down next to me and begins to butter her toast. She is soft spoken and gentle. "Your father is playing tonight, we can all go. Don't worry, we'll take good care of you," she says and strokes my black, knotted hair.

I have only known Doreen for a year, but I liked her the minute I met her. My father had been dating a younger woman after he and my mother split. She was only a few years older than Jennie, and wasn't the right match for my father on many levels. It took him a while to see it, but once he did, he left her and started dating

Doreen. Next thing we knew they were buying a house together, and a few months after that they were getting married. It happened quickly, but it was right for both of them, and I soon came to love Doreen as part of the family.

I spend the day with them, walking the dog, watching old movies, and not worrying about tomorrow, the next day, or yesterday. It feels like a vacation in the middle of chaos. Then, later, the three of us drive to a small hole-in-the-wall bar in Clarks Summit, right outside of Scranton, where my father's band is playing. It's the end of April and we are having an unusually warm weekend. I have never been here, but the minute I walk through the cold, metal door I can tell what kind of place it is. It's a bar that, because of its lack of food service, has managed to dodge Scranton's new smoking ban. It's the kind of bar where unexpected high school friends pop up like pimples.

Doreen and I are sitting at a four-top linoleum table with a metal edge, the kind you'd find in a fifties-style themed diner. We sit in silence watching my father's short arms swinging around behind his drum kit. His tongue protrudes from the corner of his mouth as he climbs further into the beat of the music. The thick smoke from the regulars planted at the long bar wafts through the skinny make-shift partition which separates their area from ours. I have left my cell phone at home, purposely. I want to disappear for a while.

Behind us sits a young, thin boy with a black knit cap and a snake of cigarette exhaust twirling from between his lips. He stares at us for a good twenty minutes before I notice him.

"Timmy?" When the music stops, I squeeze from my chair and approach him. It's Ollie's best friend, the boy who showed me a kindness at a time when no one else would. My face lights up when I recognize him.

"Amye?" his lips grow into a smile, "I thought that was you! Sit down, sit down!"

"How are you? What are you doing here?" I ask.

Timmy is more than just a boy I've gone to school with my whole life. He is Ollie's best friend. During some of the worst times in my teenage relationship with Ollie, Timmy was there for me. Sometimes he just called me to see if I was okay, other times he came to meet me when Ollie stood me up. Timmy was always the boy who picked up Ollie's slack, compensated for Ollie's lack of emotion, apologized for Ollie's actions. I always thought of him as Ollie's better half.

"I ran into your sister; she told me you were in Costa Rica. Are you back?" I asked as I lit a Newport. (It's important to note that at this time I am smoking a lot. Too much.) I shift my weight in the cheap wooden chair. I'm wearing tight jeans that cause my stomach to pop over my waistline, so I keep my purse on my lap, shielding my muffin top from Timmy's view.

"Yeah, I was mending sailboats for some local fisherman, but my money ran out." Timmy's hands are long and wide. He stretches them out across the table between us, placing one hand over mine. "You look great," he says.

"Thanks," I blush. I'm not used to men complimenting me and I instinctively wait for the 'but....'

"No, really, Aim, you look great."

The fact that Timmy has always had a crush on me was no secret, but that window of opportunity had passed a long time ago. We almost did it. We almost tried to be a couple. Once, in the ninth grade we shared a forbidden kiss in the darkness behind my parents' garage. It was sweet and soft, but in the end we decided Ollie would probably kill us both, and the idea ended there. Now, all these years later, our friendship, our connection, picks up right where it left off.

"How's your poetry? Are you still writing?"

"Great, yeah I am," I lie. I haven't written anything in years, haven't even thought of myself as a poet anymore. In my gut something sparks as I think of myself as a poet again. For a moment I imagine my life like a stretched out cassette ribbon rewinding, tucking itself back into the past. Timmy still sees me as he did in high school– talented, young, full of potential. I tug on the neckline of my low-cut sweater, suddenly feeling like I don't need to be sexy for him. My father's music floats behind us like a soundtrack for the next hour as we talk about poetry, art, music, my writing, his traveling. The one man we have in common never gets mentioned. Timmy's hazel eyes sparkle and his hands stay on mine for the better part of the time.

We are deep into a debate about Ralph Nader when my stepmother taps me on the shoulder, and the night is over. My father has played his last beat, the band is packing up, the house lights have flicked on overhead. Timmy and I hug goodbye and I leave him there, sitting at a table by himself. In the car, on the way home, my stepmother questions me.

"You guys looked awfully chummy," she teases.

"No, we're just friends. He's an old friend. He used to like me in grade school." We zip through the dark streets back to my father's house. But he's more than that. Timmy is a reminder of something good from my past.

That night as I lie once again in the spare bedroom at my father's house, I listen to the far away traffic of the interstate. I feel my heart beating slowly, calmly. I am not thinking of the mistakes I made with Jack, or Ryan, or Smithy. I'm thinking instead of Timmy, of his hands on mine, his wide smile, his enthusiasm for my writing, the small spark of energy between us. This is what it is like to have a man really see me, not just look past me. This is what it will be like someday. When I'm ready. I didn't get Timmy's phone number, or promise to look him up again; we're just friends like we've always been. But I have to say, in my brain a small glimmer of what my future could be begins to take shape.

Chapter Twenty-Three

Building a life for yourself isn't as easy as one might think. Especially when you are so bored that you're practically climbing the walls. Since moving to Wilkes-Barre, I have been unable to walk the lake everyday, which used to kill at least an hour's time. Since Smithy works with me, I've been unwilling to stay there any longer than contractually required. I'm at a loss. Luckily, I know the perfect woman to help. The following Thursday night, Pantsuit Pam makes a wonderful suggestion: *Find a hobby.* Discover something that you can throw yourself into: a new book, a craft, a garden, anything that will keep your mind off of food. Her thin lips form a perfectly straight line when she is pleased with her own advice.

"I love to garden, but it's hard on my knees," Angie, a third-shift nurse, announces.

"Then you need to pick a new love, Angie. You have all summer to lose more weight so you can garden next year. Why not pick something else in the meantime?"

Angie doesn't look happy as she slumps back into the aluminum chair that is straining to contain her. We are in our semi-circle, with Pantsuit Pam as the nucleus.

"How many of you have ever wanted to do something that you keep putting off until the weight is gone?" Pantsuit Pam asks. The crowd buzzes with agreement and recognition. "But you never do it, do you," she continues "because the weight is never gone. Your whole life is on hold until that one moment when suddenly you wake up and you are a skinny person."

As Pantsuit Pam speaks I replay all of the things I have put off in my life "until I lose the weight." First on that list was leaving Jack. Now, he's gone. Behind that is a litany of activities I have convinced myself I will probably never perform: climb a mountain, hike the Appalachian trail, pose for a family portrait, kiss someone under the Eiffel Tower, join The Peace Corps, learn to play guitar, and of course, have a baby.

For years I have been telling myself that Jack and my weight were the only two things separating me from a life of non-stop excitement and fulfillment. Yet, here I am, divorced and sixty-seven pounds lighter, and my life is still pretty much what it was. Yes, I have moved. Yes, I have been promoted at work. But the bottom line is that I have not traveled and I have not tried anything outside of my comfort zone. I am still selling my soul every day working for a company I loathe.

"This is your homework," Pantsuit Pam tells us, "Go do something new this week. And I'll see you back here next week, happy and lighter!"

Normally, I would shrug off such a suggestion, convinced I was too busy to start a new project. But the boredom is seeping into my skin, pounding away at my sanity like a jackhammer. I could always go to a bar. That option is always there. But I am tired of sitting in bars and crying over boys. I need to do something meaningful, something important. I need to push myself. I need to do what my father suggested and start creating a home within myself.

I decide to go to downtown Scranton, where I find a small music shop and purchase a used acoustic guitar for one hundred dollars. It is beautiful: black with a pearl inlay. I sit on a folding chair, rest her on my thighs, and strum the strings. I feel like a mother holding her newborn baby. I have no idea how to play, but I know I can learn.

After I hand over my hundred dollars, a tall man with salt and pepper hair and a nose the size of a mountain slides my new instrument across the counter with my receipt.

"Do you know how to play?" he asks.

"Nope."

"We have lessons available, you know."

"I know. I can't afford them," I whisper.

He looks me up and down for what feels like five minutes. I can't tell if he finds me attractive or pathetic. "Here, take this. You can have it," he whispers back and slides a glossy white book across the glass countertop. It's a thin book called *How to Play the Guitar*. On the cover, a young man is on his knees and slamming his head towards the ground and his hair is a cascade of blonde falling from the sky above him. He is jamming out, I suppose.

For the next few weeks, I do exactly as Pantsuit Pam suggests. I throw myself into that guitar. I do nothing but sit on my couch and memorize chords. A, G, E minor, I know them all within seven days. "Brown-Eyed Girl" is the first song I learn, although most beginners start with Tom Petty. I play that song a million times, until calluses form on my left hand from pressing on the strings. Every night I rush home from work, open my book, and play until the sun slips from the sky.

A few guys from work and from my building play as well, and soon we start to form an informal practice group. They come to my apartment after dinner, and we play for hours. There are usually five of us, all with guitars on our laps, picks in our hands, and warming beers on the floor next to us. Joe, my friend from down the street, is trained both classically and traditionally. The first time I hear him play his classical guitar, his thin fingers climbing like spiders lightly over the silk strings, it's so beautiful and gentle that I consider sleeping with him. But twenty minutes later, he is babbling on and on about how great George Bush is and my attraction blinks off like the no smoking sign on an airplane.

Sergio lives on the third floor in my building. He is also classically trained, and much more talented than any one of us. He is tall and slim with hair down to the middle of his back. He is madly in love with his wife, Heather, a vegan, a poet, and a transplant from California. Neither one of them have jobs, yet they have a child and manage to live on their own. Sometimes Sergio brings the baby and plops him in a bouncy chair in the corner of my living room. The baby, a boy named Alto, doesn't make a sound.

Then there's Smithy. My obsession with him has waned enough that when he joins our group, I am not tempted in the least to invite him to stay. The pattern has been broken, the routine has changed. But that does not sit well with him and despite having a new girlfriend, he still follows me into the kitchen, runs his hand up the small of my back, and pours sexual innuendo into my ears. I brush him off and move forward, anxious to get back to my guitar and the new chord progression we are working on.

Finally there's Aaron. A strikingly handsome boy who works hard, owns his own house, and on paper is the perfect catch. The only problem is that he knows it. When he plays, his tongue juts from the corner of his lips, his blue eyes narrow, and his broad wrists float up and down the fret board effortlessly. He's beautiful to watch and to listen to. He is a prize at the bottom of a cereal box, a five-dollar bill lying on the ground with no one around, but he is cocky and arrogant. He flirts with me, smells delicious, touches my face when we talk, and then proceeds to tells me how beautiful I'd be...if I lost weight. Still, I lose my inhibitions one night and end up in his bed. Miraculously, I am able to shrug it off and continue on like it never happened. Partly because I don't want to hear his admission of regret, and partly because I have almost no memory of the event.

These guitar parties happen all summer long. There are nights when our five instruments fall into harmony like a feather floating easily to the floor. Then, there are times when we drink too much and our timing tangles with laughter. We are a symphony of mismatched souls who mesh to form a chorus of belonging. On a particularly balmy night, I well up with tears as I walk back into the living room and watch my new friends playing "Hallelujah" by Leonard Cohen. Sergio is singing as Joe, Smithy, and Aaron strum long, narrow notes lightly behind him. Sergio's voice is glass, fragile and strong at the same time. His voice is a memory, a moment I will swim back to when I am drowning in pain. Inside of me a calm is starting to expand. These friends are mine. This apartment is mine. This love of music is mine. This is my own life, taking shape around me.

Chapter Twenty-Four

By midsummer, the crowd of women who have come to hear Pantsuit Pam's advice has dwindled. What used to be a packed, standing-room-only kind of crowd only weeks ago is now back down to the numbers we started with: six, maybe seven.

This was to be expected, Sherri with an i explains to me before the meeting. We just weighed in, me dropping another 2.6, her dropping 1.4. The smiles on our faces are broad and hard to contain. We slip our sandals back over our thick cotton socks, retrieve our books from Joan, and walk in solidarity into the meeting room. We are a choreographed duo, dancing our way through this Points system. We are tangoing through temptation, together.

"Watch, no one will be here tonight," Sherri says from the side of her mouth after we take our places in the crescent moon of aluminum.

"Why not?" I ask. I had noticed a decline in numbers recently, but assumed it was due to the constant rain, or the downturn in the economy.

"It's almost summer," she says casually, "the New Year's resolutions have run their course."

Suddenly, all of my failed resolutions are a montage in my memory. The broken promises, the failed starts, and the unrealized dreams. Every year, as the calendar flipped from December to January, a new beginning was laid out before me. A reset. A redo. And I always fell into the trap. *This will be the year. I will get to that coveted place, I will be skinny.* This year will be the year that all of my troubles will dissipate, fall off like extra pounds, shrivel up and die. I would begin an exercise regimen, stock my cabinets full of fruits and vegetables, and announce to the world that the fat Amye would be gone by mid-year, September at the latest.

And my newfound motivation would last…for a while. Five, six, maybe even seven pounds would drop from my body quickly in response to the suddenly-imposed starvation. But sure enough, as spring began to find its way to the surface, my will would dissolve and my self-control would melt into the ground and disappear with the winter snow. I wonder now if people looked at my failed efforts like Sherri with an i looked at the failed efforts of others. Did they think I was a fool? A pig who could not control herself? A pathetic loser?

A spark of guilt is igniting inside of me. I can't help but cringe when I think of all the people I have disappointed over the years. My parents, especially. Their hopes riding high with each announcement of my upcoming attempt to be skinny. When I was fourteen or fifteen, the exact timeline is a blur, my mother hired a nutritionist to plan my meals. He and I sat at my kitchen table in comfortable padded chairs and discussed carbohydrates, fats, and calories. With his thick, hairy hands, he mapped out on a sheet of graph paper what I would be allowed to eat for breakfast: cereal with skim milk, an English muffin with apple butter, or cottage cheese and fresh fruit. Suggested dinner ideas included: grilled chicken breast, salmon, poached eggs, lean steak. I remember thinking, *I'm fifteen, where the fuck am I going to get salmon?*

Years later, I'm away at school. I lose some weight. Not much, but enough that I need new pants. My father wires me a hundred dollars almost immediately, excitement in his voice as he confirms my receipt of the funds. *I will gladly help you out for smaller clothes*, he says with a giggle in his throat. I buy two pairs of size sixteen jeans, only to outgrow them again in a month.

Then I was home, engaged, married, fat. Really, really fat. I remember lying in bed at night year after year, staring at the cracked white ceiling, swearing that tomorrow will be different. *I will start again, I will get there, I will do it. Jack will fall in love with me again when I'm skinny.* My resolve was so strong during those night time hours, the willpower so close and within reach, as I lay there with my belly still bulging from dinner. *I can do this. I can get there.*

Then, the inevitable. No one comes right out and

acknowledges the end. No one says the word: failed. My declarations of a new diet are wiped from our memories like rain off a windshield, gone. We act like we don't remember. My parents never speak of my broken commitments, but I can see it in their eyes. The sadness, the deflated dreams, the small glimmer of hope slowly fading. I know, because it's dwindling inside of me as well.

Now, listening to Sherri with an i predicting failure for our fellow sisters in arms, my heart goes out to those who have fallen away. I know what they will be thinking as they stare at their ceilings tonight. *Tomorrow is a new day. I will begin again, tomorrow.*

But as much as I miss and sympathize with our drop-outs, I refuse to join them. I have lost seventy pounds and it feels wonderful. I have begun working the program the right way, and have been rewarded graciously. I have become obsessed with lying on my bed and running my hands up and down my new body. My chins are tightening, my hip bones are emerging, and I have a collarbone! It's as if a glacier is melting to reveal the beautiful city that had always remained hidden underneath. And for the first time in my entire life, I feel like I am over the hump, past the point of no return. I am finally on the other side of fat.

"Well, don't worry," I whisper back to Sherri with an i, "I'm not going anywhere."

And for the first time in my life, I believe that.

Chapter Twenty-Five

Jennie and I are in Manhattan, having just exited the 7 Train and scurrying towards daylight through a massive underground walkway that promises to spit us out onto 42nd Street. My sister has only been living here for four months, but she blends right in. She skips the steps two at a time. She slinks to the right when she should, hugging the smooth white subway tile which hasn't been its original color in probably close to sixty years. She snubs the homeless man playing an old guitar with only three strings.

I cannot help but stare. He is blacker than anyone I have ever seen. His skin is mud. His eyes are charcoal. His hands, almost yellow on the bottoms, strum across the strings. His voice slips out of his throat almost by accident, but it's beautiful. I stop to watch him and am immediately hit from behind by a stroller wheel, followed by a purse, two guys speaking Arabic, a cane, three backpacks, and finally, my sister who has circled back for me on a recon mission.

"Come on, keep moving," she instructs me.

The tunnel smells like hot garbage soup. It's sweat and vomit and urine all at once. People walk in ropes. The right is heading towards the street. The left is descending further underground. We move so fast it looks like we are standing still. We are a machine. We create a hum. We are gears sliding back and forth under dim lights and hundred-story buildings overhead.

Twenty minutes ago, we were on the 7 train from Queens into Manhattan. We were passing an old warehouse with busted out windows that had been taken over by artists as loft space. The shell of the building was covered in graffiti art. Not tags, not anti-Bush sentiments, but actual art. Twenty-foot-high portraits of Snoop Dogg and Batman sat next to volcanoes spewing body parts and suns setting behind silver clouds.

"It's majestic," Jennie pointed out. She sat across from me on the sleek air- conditioned train.

"Yeah, it's awesome. Look at the Al Pacino! It looks just like him!" I shouted over the metallic squeal surrounding us.

"No," she said, "I mean what the artists are doing. They're taking industry and making it their own; taking it back and making it work for them."

I can't keep up with her. I pant and huff and puff my way through the crowds. The tourists are the ones who stop right in the middle of the procession, Jennie told me when I first arrived. The important thing was to keep moving. That seems to be the rule in this city of a million distractions: keep moving. Moving about the city, navigating its subway system, transferring trains, and calling cars. It's what consumes those who live here. It becomes a battle within yourself to find the most efficient way to travel to your destination. Jennie and her friends spend up to an hour plotting their route before they even leave the house.

We find an exit and climb the twenty or so steps from the tunnel out onto 42nd street. Around us are a million people from every nook and cranny of the country. Lights flash, horns blare, profanity floats through the air tangled with exhaust and expensive perfume. Jennie stares at the city around her. We have our father's hair color, jet black, almost blue in the sun. Jennie's hair frames her face, poker straight with severe bangs. She wears jeans and long sleeves even when it's eighty degrees outside, as most locals do. She has long earrings, longer than most necklaces I've seen. They feather out into delicate silver fans that cascade down into waterfalls over her angular shoulder blades. Her eyes are tar balls, dark and slippery, staring lustfully at the buildings around her. She is one of them. She is a New Yorker. She is a mural of culture and diversity. She has liquefied into the melting pot of Manhattan. She has heard its call, felt its pull, and forgotten us. And I realize, I have lost her yet again, just as I had so many times throughout our lives together.

Jennie and Josh have settled their lives in Greenpoint. It is a part of Brooklyn that has seen better days. If you ask her, this neighborhood is on the brink of something bigger. It's Chelsea waiting to happen, SoHo in its infancy. To me, it looks like a street from Bosnia in the 1990s. The bums on the corner have set up shanties made from weakened cardboard boxes, old flannel shirts, and discolored newspapers. Their urine streaks and stains the brick exterior of the building behind them. The cops, the social workers, the bleeding hearts with no money, walk right past them. No one complains out loud. After all, it's their home now too.

The walk to the bar is long and hot. The summer air lies on our backs like satchels full of wet, damp blankets. I pretend not to feel it. I am on a mission to forget about the boys who have hurt me. To start over, again. I am also here to show off my new body. I have lost over eighty pounds. I have shed a whole person, or at least a very hungry supermodel. And now, I'm walking down Greenpoint Avenue in the middle of the night with my sister, and for the first time in my life, I am within reach of her weight. I am normal. The last time I weighed this much I was in ninth grade, just off a bout with mono.

"Two Hefeweizens please," Jennie whispers to the bartender.

"And a shot of Jager," I add.

In her neighborhood, as in most of the boroughs, you can whisper in a bar and still be heard. There are no local bands with out of tune instruments or a whining lead singer. People are not raising voices to be heard over a large neon jukebox that plays a variety of Bon Jovi music. The bars here are laid back and peaceful. They are places of Zen. They only get loud towards the end of the night, when people are debating the best routes to travel home.

We are in a bar called The Pencil Factory. It's a small space with only candles to provide the lighting. The tables, of which there are only four, are large slabs of unfinished wood. I run my hands over our table repeatedly, almost consumed with trying to get a sliver. There are no chairs only benches. The floor is dusty and dirty and looks like it belongs in a western saloon. I would not be completely shocked if someone walked through the plate glass door wearing chaps.

Jennie and I sit and watch the people around us. I am fascinated by their casual nature. One girl wears what looks like pajamas as she leans in and whispers to a man wearing shorts and no shirt. A couple by the door have brought their dog, a large white mutt who sleeps with his slobbering mouth on the girl's sandaled foot. They are at ease in this space.

Twenty-five minutes and three beers later, the room is

beginning to spin, my legs are starting to feel warm and fuzzy, and my lips long for the taste of a menthol cigarette.

"I'm going for a smoke," I say and leave Jennie, her face illuminated only by the screen on her Blackberry.

The Pencil Factory is on a corner with a stop sign right in front. I am the only smoker, ostracized to the street by the no-smoking-in-bars law that has made being in a bar in New York City breathable again. I am not fearful as I stand there by myself with a thin line of white exhaust leaking from my lips. I do not flinch when a group of young men, strong and imposing, walk past me with their eyes locked on my breasts. I do not care that the nearest street light is a block away, and the only illumination I have comes from the neon beer advertisements in the windows behind me. The door to the bar stays open at my back, another oddity you would never find in Scranton. It's inviting and warm.

Before I can finish my smoke, a large black SUV pulls to the stop sign in front of me. The four guys inside wear bandanas drenched with sweat and are talking over loud music when they spot me standing on the corner in my short skirt and tight top. For what feels like five whole minutes, I enjoy them looking at me, objectifying me, imagining me naked, having their way with me. I imagine if I were more daring I might go home with one of them, let him ravish me, and sneak out in the morning before daybreak. I imagine if they were in the bar behind me, I might let one buy me a drink, or pretend to be too drunk to notice his hands on my breasts. I stand there, eight eyes on me, feeling as brazen as I have ever felt, when the passenger in the front sticks his head out the window and, with the whole bar listening through the open door behind me yells at the top of his lungs.

"WOW! That's a whale even I would fuck!"

Then, just like that, they are gone. My cigarette falls to the ground, my stomach flips. I suck in the night air and regain my composure. I want to chase after them, to explain to them that I have *lost* weight. I could show them a before and after picture. "See?

126

See how fat I used to be? 265 pounds! That was fat! This, 183, this is not fat! Trust me!" I would force them to look. I would show them my stomach, the stretch marks, the hanging skin, the proof of a fatter existence. Then, maybe I would kill one of them, stab him to death with a shard of glass after I bust their windows out. Maybe I could light their fancy SUV on fire, or find out where they live and kill their pets.

"What happened? You okay?" Jennie asks emerging from the bar.

"I'm fine," I answer choking back tears, and walk a straight line back to our table without a wiggle in my hips.

The next night, I am on a bus cutting through the Pennsylvania mountains like a yo-yo being sucked back onto its string, heading towards Scranton. It's pitch black around me. I'm slumped against the soft fabric of my seat, and all I can think about is those boys in that SUV. Months ago, a comment like that would have crushed me. It would have sent me head first into a bottomless bag of fast food and I would not have come out until I was fifteen pounds heavier and up two pant sizes. Now, I feel *okay*. I'm not a whale. Sure, maybe compared to Jennie or most New Yorkers who are ungodly thin, but compared to last year's Amye, I'm doing well. I'm working hard, I'm working towards something. I'm not going to let a bunch of assholes destroy me, and I'm not going to destroy myself. Not anymore.

Chapter Twenty-Six

It's a Thursday night in August and Pantsuit Pam is asking us to review our internal dialogue. She asks us to shout out the things we tell ourselves when we look in the mirror. "One, two, three, go!" she says. What follows, is a barrage of insults and harsh criticisms.

I'm a fuck up. I'm fat. I'm ugly. No one will ever love me. I will screw everything up. If anyone ever did love me, they will be sorely disappointed when

127

they discover who I really am. I'm a loser. People see right through me. I have a fat ass. My thighs shake when I walk. I have thirty chins. My face looks like a balloon. I never want to be seen in public. I hate how I look, breathe, feel, smell. I want people to see me, but no one ever will. Who am I kidding? I'm disgusting, out of control, horrid.

I look around the room. The women saying these horrible things are all staring at the ceiling, their eyes rolling back into their fat faces like marbles getting rolled into bread dough. We are ashamed; embarrassed of the way we talk to ourselves. Pam pulls a chair from the correct formation and sits down. She leans her long, thin body forward and plants her elbows on her knees.

"Listen to yourselves," she says with a twinge of emotion in her tone, "Listen to what you are saying to yourselves."

The room goes silent.

"It's as if we feel like we don't deserve to have confidence. Why? Why don't we deserve that?" Pam asks.

No one says a word.

"Amye," Pam looks at me, "Would you ever say any of the things you've just heard, to anyone else in your life, anyone else in this room for that matter?"

"No. Never."

"Angie, think about your worst enemy," Pantsuit Pam instructs. Angie closes her puffy eyelids. "Now, would you say any of those things to that person?"

"Probably not," Angie mutters.

"Think about this ladies," Pam lowers her face and juts her neck out. Her eyes narrow in on us. "You give your worst enemies more respect than you give yourselves. What is wrong with that picture?"

The seven of us mumble in agreement and shift uncomfortably in our chairs. We are like children caught with our hand in the cookie jar. We are being scolded.

"This is called self-sabotage. If this is how you feel about yourself, can you imagine the image you are projecting to others?"

128

Pam allows the silence to hover over us for a few moments before she rises and starts writing on the board. "Tonight, when you go home, I want you to write down ten positive things about yourself," she says. "Write them on a sheet of paper and tape that list somewhere you will see it every morning. Those ten things will be your new inner dialogue. The beginning of a new and healthier relationship with yourself."

I cannot wait. *Pantsuit Pam is a goddamn genius.* In the car, I flip on a dome light, pull a bank envelope from my purse and begin my list. All of the good things I want to say about myself are easily accessible. I have been accumulating them for years. Only, they currently reside in the folder in my brain marked: "Things I want someone else to see in me." Right thoughts, wrong folder.

The Ten Things I Like About Myself
1. I have pretty eyes.
2. I am kind.
3. I am smart.
4. I have nice, petite hands.
5. I am good with money. (Lame).
6. I can play guitar.
7. I am a good friend.
8. I am a good sister.
9. I can write well.

Before I can finish my list, I hear what sounds like faint sobs coming from the dark parking lot around me. I roll my window down further. Yes, there it is again. For a few seconds I wonder if I should jump out, look around, and investigate the noise. But I'm too nervous. It's dark and late, and I am in no way capable of defending myself against a crazy person.

Turns out, I don't have to look far. Across the hood of my car, as I click on my headlights, they shine on a heavy young woman sitting in her driver's seat and crying into her hands. I recognize her dark curls and bright pink top. She is one of us. A newbie to the program, she has been here once or twice, at the most. When my headlights penetrate her solace, she jerks her head up and stares at me. Her bright red cheeks are slick and shiny. There are tears still perched in the corners of her eyes. We sit there, only feet apart, our bumpers practically touching, staring at one another. We are connected by an ocean of steel.

My instinct is to go to her, to cradle her in my arms, and comfort one of my own. I want to tell her that it's not as hard as she thinks, not as far away as she imagines, and not as unreachable as she tells herself. But the stare in her eyes tells me she is not in the mood for my pep talk. Her brow begins to furrow as her glare intensifies. Suddenly, I am uncomfortable. Her lips straighten, her nostrils flare. She is angry with me, yet I cannot understand for what reason. I pull out of the parking lot and leave her in the blackness.

Then, about two blocks down the road, it hits me. *Oh my God. She thinks I am one of them.* I have lost over eighty pounds. I am much thinner than I was, but I am not *skinny*…am I? I mean, I guess when you compare numbers, 183 up against what I started with, 265, I could comparably be considered skinny (er). My eyes dart from the road to the rearview mirror and back again. I barely recognize myself. One chin, cheekbones, a narrow nose.

I am not one of those skinny girls, I say out loud. I am not one of those girls who never has to think about her weight, who can live a normal life without counting every fucking morsel of food she puts in her mouth. I will never be the girl in the center of a flock of boys. I will never be able to pull off halter tops or go braless on hot summer days. I am one of *us*. No matter what my size, I am one of *us*. A fat girl. I pull my car to the side of the road, fish my list out of my purse and finish writing:

10. I am a *fucking* fat girl, and I am okay with that.

Pantsuit Pam is right. We are what we say we are, and I am proud to say that I am a fat girl. My weight loss has not come without scars. I have been humiliated most of my adult life. I have had to work so hard at being accepted, so sweet and nice, always overcompensating for the lack of aesthetic on the outside. I have been through the war, and have come out on the other side. But, no matter what my size, I will always be one of them. I will always remember what it feels like to be called names, called out, or not called back because of my size. I will always be able to feel the heat on the rails of self-loathing. But with these women, this group of astonishingly supportive women, I will be okay. I will make it through. *Hang on,* I want to tell her, *hang on. You will become one of us. We will accept you.*

part three

Chapter Twenty-Seven

By late summer, I am within ten pounds of my goal, and the mere foreshadowing of that moment, standing on the scale and seeing my magical number, has transformed me into the perfect dieter. Suddenly, I have become the nutrition Nazi. I live and breathe the plan. Since moving to Wilkes-Barre, I've had a hard time making it up to Lake Scranton every day, so I join the local YMCA and work out for one hour every day after work. I suck down fruits and vegetables like a compost machine. I stop drinking almost altogether, not willing to "waste the points" on a beer or a glass of wine. I am beyond dedicated. I am a hardcore motherfucker. If I could afford it, I'd get WW tattooed on my forearm.

I have an idea, I tell Joe, Sergio, and Aaron one night after we've strummed our last song and are buckling up our guitars. *I want to train to run a marathon.* They look at me like I'm nuts and continue arguing politics. (Joe, the token Republican, is usually in the minority when such arguments break out.)

But I'm serious. I want to run a marathon. I feel a new sense of life has been breathed into me. I feel like a paraplegic who has just gotten out of her wheelchair for the first time. I want to run, to sweat, and to push myself to the brink of exhaustion. Yes, losing ninety pounds has made me look better, but I never could have imagined how it would make me *feel.* Suddenly the little things I could never do before are possible. I can go to amusement parks and not worry about the bar closing over my stomach. I can lie in bed and read a book without having to prop two pillows under my head. I can sit on the floor with my legs crossed for hours without *anything* feeling numb. I can wear shorts without worrying if my thighs will rub together and chafe.

If you decide to run a marathon, I will be there, Sergio whispers in my ear as he leaves. I smile. Of course he will. He's become a wonderful friend through all of this. He and his wife, Heather, have been excellent influences on my diet and my life. They eat organically, they are sober most of the time, and they honestly care about their health. I spend most of the summer upstairs at their third-floor apartment. From Heather, I learn how to prepare an eggplant twelve different ways. From Sergio, I learn how to use a capo to make the bar chords easier to play. On the fourth of July, the three of us walk down to the Market Street Bridge, with baby Alto on Heather's back. We stand against the concrete pillars and watch as fireworks of every hue pop against the sky like shattering glass. When the crowd swells, Heather signals for me to lean against her. And I do. But perhaps the most important contribution to my life that Heather and Sergio make comes on a Friday after dinner.

"I have something for you," Sergio announces and slides from his chair, disappearing down the hallway into the bedroom. "Wait just a minute, I'm getting it!" his voice is an audible trail behind him.

Outside there is a chorus of crickets harmonizing on the small patch of woods behind our building. The kitchen is a melody of smells. Heather has made grilled eggplant in balsamic vinegar (2 points), and a delicious salad (3 points). *I can't believe these people. They eat like birds*, I first thought when I broke bread at their table. But I'm starting to realize something. This is how *normal* people eat.

Sergio emerges with a book. He sits back down, slams the book on the table and slides it towards me. His long brown hair frames his face like curtains. His hands are long and slender, with a yarn bracelet wrapped around his wrist. Heather is breast feeding the baby across from us. She makes no attempt to conceal her breast; it's just out there, like another dinner guest. She smiles as I pick up the present and read the cover: *Writing Down the Bones, Freeing the Writer Within.*

"Now, why don't you start writing some of those poems you're always telling us about?" Sergio says.

The baby coos and my eyes are hammocks filled with years of tears. I look around the table at my friends. This is what I've always wanted my life to look like. For a moment I am stuck to the ceiling, my back pressed against the high white swirled plaster. Below I see myself as I have always wanted to, surrounded by warm people who love me and love each other; people who are filled with brightness. "This is the most thoughtful thing anyone has ever done for me," I say.

Later, when I am back in my apartment, with the lights low and the air thick with cigarette smoke, it is as if a volcano has erupted inside of me. I write three poems within minutes of one another. They pour straight from my gut. They're all riddled with hyperbole and way too close to my pain to even make sense, but it's a start. It's the most I've written in as long as I can remember, and the feeling of plucking a metaphor from the air reminds me of who I have always wanted to be. This is a gift that I will never be able to repay.

Chapter Twenty-Eight

The relationship with my scale is as precarious as two teenagers in heat. Sure, as long as everyone is doing what they're told and playing by the rules, it's all butterflies and hand jobs. But inevitably, someone wanders outside the lines, the mutual trust is broken, someone's head swivels, and the next thing you know it's all death threats and restraining orders. But I can't walk away. I am tethered to this uncertainty. This is my life as a fat girl. This is the life of someone trying so desperately to be something else. To be thin. To be normal. To be accepted. To be anything but what we are. We can turn on a dime. We can flip the switch from rage to sage in five seconds flat. And it all depends on one thing: that smooth, slick bastard of a scale in the corner of my bathroom.

There are only thirty-seven steps between my bed and my scale. I know this, because every morning, before my eyes even fully open, I take that journey. Some days, when I have been good the night before, and I can feel my skin loose and a pocket of air under my feet, the walk is more of a skip. It's a journey made with baited breath, with hopes high and fingers crossed. It's like having a boy slip his hand under your shirt for the first time, or sneaking out with your girlfriends at three o'clock in the morning.

Then, there are nights when I fuck up. When I slip and allow a hot fudge sundae or a dozen 10-cent garlic parmesan wings past my lips and the next morning my skin feels like sausage casing stretched over layers of fat and gristle and I can barely drag my pork loin legs to the floor. Those are the mornings when the world is heavy and nothing comes easy. Those are the mornings when I have to stop myself from smashing my scale into a billion pieces with a sledgehammer and lying on the ground while the remaining shards float down over me like ash.

It all starts with a routine, a series of rituals I perform before the actual weighing can commence. I climb from the warmth of my bed, walk those thirty-seven steps across my tattered Berber carpet, empty my bladder of every last drip drop, strip off every last inch of clothing, exhale every last bit of breath from my lungs, and slide my bare feet onto the scale's belly. I am a slave reporting to my master. I am a prisoner of the war within myself. A war that, since its inception, has divided, conquered, and crushed my self esteem, my sense of self, and all the parts of my brain that those skinny, regular girls have intact.

But on a cold September morning in my school house loft, the hundred years war inside of me screeches to a halt. I begin that thirty seven step journey, as I always do, but today I know immediately that something is different. My steps are lighter. The air smells sweeter. The birds outside my window are chirping a Beach Boys tune. Through my window burns the light of a thousand suns. There is something special about this day. I close my eyes and begin the routine: pee, strip, exhale, pee again (just in case). My feet stick to the white plastic and nothing in the world moves, not even my heart, as the cherry red needle begins its ascent in the three inch wide window. *One hundred, one twenty, one thirty*, impossible numbers, numbers I will only someday dream about are left in the dust as the red pioneer forges forward. *One forty, one fifty, one sixty*, the pace begins to slow, *one sixty two, one sixty three*, a plunge towards *one seventy*, then a ping pong back. Finally, the needle settles. *One sixty-five.* Goal. I have reached my goal.

Suddenly, the world is thrust back into motion. My heart bursts with blood, breath blows back into my lungs, my body shakes, and my eyes well up. I step from the scale, stand against the white wall, and slide to the ground. I pull my knees in tight to my chest and sob. Almost a year ago, I was divorced and morbidly obese. I was heartbroken and scared. I was alone and not sure if I would ever be okay, ever again. I cried every night for weeks, I drank too much, made really bad decisions, wore some questionable clothing, and smoked like a car wreck. And then, maybe because of some cosmic plan or just a really good deal on the joining fee, I tumbled like a stone into a Weight Watcher's meeting and wrote 165 in that little box marked: GOAL.

And now, that number is tangible. I can feel it poking into my newly discovered rib cage, brushing against my protruding collarbones, pressing against my slimming thighs. I have made it. I have gotten here. I haven't achieved very many things in my life. I have a dozen "before" pictures, but never an "after." I never ran a marathon, competed seriously for and landed a job, birthed a child, or finished Super Mario Brothers 3, but *this* is something I've *done*. I've lost a hundred pounds, finally, and for real. In that moment, it is as if a river has been released inside of me, and floating down that river are the moments I remember most about being fat: Being rejected by boys, the whispers of coworkers at work, the constant disappointment on my parents' faces, Jack walking out the door.

Then, there is a moment so raw and painful I have to close my eyes as it floats to the surface. At the absolute lowest point in my life, when I felt nothing but FAT and I could barely stand to look at myself, I put my body into a tub of hot water and I sank. I sank until the suds covered my bulging belly and breasts, until my three chins were submerged. I sank until the steaming liquid slipped into my ears, pulled my hair, and wrapped around my mouth. Down, down, down. I closed my eyes, and felt myself slip under. I wasn't scared. I was relieved. I pressed the sides of the tub, forcing my body to stay submerged. I wanted to disappear from the planet, to wash away what I was. To erase the stain of me. Now, on this cool September morning, all of those painful memories flop around on my bathroom floor, like waterless fish, gasping for air.

I want to tell the world about my accomplishment. I want to fling open the windows of my loft apartment and scream until the little dangly thing at the back of my throat wears raw red. I want to be one of those girls that has something, *anything* to brag about. Instead, I fill my cracked plastic bathtub with hot water and slip into the soapy white basin. All these years later, the water covers my whole body effortlessly. I close my eyes, feel the warmth against my skin and remember what it was like, all those years ago, to feel an urge to let go and slip under the slick skin of the water. *I am so far from that place*, I think to myself. *I am floating.*

Chapter Twenty-Nine

The air pocket under my feet continues the next night as I walk through the parking lot of the IBEW building. Others who are getting out of their cars, searching for their food diaries, or tucking jiggling key rings into oversized leather purses can smell it on me as

I walk by. It is the scent of success, the scent of victory. I cannot wipe the smile from my lips. It is as if it has been tattooed or branded onto my face. The glass doors seem to part automatically as I approach, and the line of waiting overweight women seems to split up the middle as I enter the long, wood-paneled hallway.

These women, they recognize the look: the sight of someone who has crawled through the long dark tunnel of obesity and has emerged into the warm, waiting sunlight on the other side. They want to be happy for me, to cheer me on, to lift their hands high in the air and connect with mine. But they can't. They are still in that tunnel, they are still crawling, scraping their knees, forging ahead, and I represent what they want. They would kill me right now with their bare hands if they thought they could get away with it. I know this so well, because as recently as one week ago, I was one of them.

Once inside, Joan and Pantsuit Pam make quite the big deal over my accomplishment. Even though I have not reached my program goal, the impossible number Pam would like to see appear in my scale's window, a member losing a hundred pounds is quite the big hullabaloo. The first five to ten minutes of a meeting are always reserved for "business." This means anything from announcing program changes to welcoming new members into our circle. Pam delights in these moments; it is all of her hard work, paid off. I can't remember if the group leaders are paid, and if they are I'm sure it's a minimal amount. But I imagine her reward comes in moments like this: me standing and a room full of my peers applauding me.

"A hundred pounds!" Pam reiterates. *If she can do it, you can too. Believe me,* is what she's really saying. *Look! I know how to do this! I can motivate you, too!*

After I stood on the scale and the metal weight skidded to a stop at 165, Nervous Joan gasped for air. Then, without missing a beat, proceeded to announce my accomplishment to the room. I received a bunch of goodies: another link for my brushed silver keychain, a coupon for two dollars off a box of Weight Watcher's brand snacks, and the eternal admiration of the support staff.

I'd be lying if I said it didn't feel good. I have never really achieved anything of this magnitude before. Jennie was the smart one, she won all of the awards, was accepted into the Gifted Program at school, and later she even joined Mensa. She was also the pretty one and the skinny one. I stood in her shadow for most of my life. Then, Georgia came into my life, and she became the even prettier one. Men flocked to her like she had magnets in her hips. I was always invisible. But today in front of Pam and my portly peers, I am special.

I look around at these women, my support group, and I want to hug them all, even though I know their admiration is nine parts jealousy and one part genuine. But before this moment, when I was down there in the pits with them, they were sisters to me. They have been a net, scaffolding under my battle for metabolic sobriety for almost a year, and I couldn't be more grateful for each and every one of them. We may not be friends in the outside world, but the bond we share inside of these four walls is intense and covers us like a web.

Later, after the buzz surrounding my loss dies down, Pantsuit Pam asks us about the future. Not the future like flying cars and robot mail men, but about my future. About two years from now, three years from now, or ten years from now. Immediately, the room starts to buzz like a giant bee hive with women old and young throwing numbers out like day traders on the floor of the New York Stock Exchange. *Fifty, seventy, twenty-three, one-hundred*, pounds lost, pounds forgotten, pounds discarded. Smiles are painted all over our chubby faces as we dream about being slender, thin, not fat. But then Pam announces the caveat: she isn't talking about weight.

"Your lives right now," Pam explains, "are about losing weight. But once you achieve your goal, what will your lives be about then? It's important that you set other goals for yourself. If you have nothing, you risk falling backwards, filling your time with eating."

She's right. I imagine myself teetering on the edge of a cliff, my heels halfway into the open air, with only darkness and the unknown sprawled out before me. It would be so easy, so calming, to close my eyes and feel my body like a feather floating backwards into the open sky, and knowing these women will be there to catch me when I near the ground. But there will be a day when they will not be there with arms outstretched and baited breath, simply waiting for the weight of me.

And that's the day Pam is preparing us for. The day when she will push us like reluctant birds from this comfortable nest she has created around us. When that day comes, she wants us to have a dream, something to wish for and to strive towards. She wants us to construct an intricate system of support around the fragile construct of our weight loss that will survive anything. A net that will ensure we stay on the right path, the path leading to health. While I've spent a lot of time and energy creating a life for myself, I never stopped to think beyond the here and now. What will my future look like? Where will I be in five years? "This is your homework," she says, "think about the vast landscape before you. Where do you want it to lead?"

Chapter Thirty

Georgia's mother will survive. The doctors cut her open like a can of tuna fish, took out all of the black, putrid parts, and sewed her back up. Only now, she will have a plastic bag permanently attached to her; a bag that will always be slightly filled, hanging like an extra organ under her clothes close to her hip. But it could have been worse. It could have been so much worse. Georgia had not prepared for that, but I had. Ready at any moment to find my phone illuminated with her number and her screaming voice at the other end. I had imagined the funeral, and had even written the eulogy in my head.

But I was wrong, and I'm thrilled. News of her mother's

victory over cancer brings Georgia to a new calm. A new respect for the fragility of life.

"I'm going to try for another baby," she tells me one night as we sit sipping margaritas at La Tolteca.

"What?" The news hits me from behind like a club.

"I want to have another baby."

I say nothing and slurp the strawberry and tequila down as I digest the news. The orange-tiled table between us grows smaller and I wish for a minute that I could slide down her straw into her throat and become her. Fertile, able to create life at a moment's whim.

"But...what about? I mean, are you sure you want to..." I stammer.

"What? Amye, what are you trying to say?" The tension in her voice is growing.

"Well, no offense but, doesn't your marriage already suck? I mean it's going to be harder than hell to get out of that relationship with *two* kids."

What about all of the plans we've made? I want to say. *The circles we've walked around the lake, dreaming of being free? What about the life you always wanted, a life with a better man? What are you doing to yourself?*

"Aim, it's not that easy. When you have kids, you just can't pack up and leave," Georgia looks down at her margarita and plays with the straw, stabbing at the frozen strawberries.

In that moment, I am so grateful that I was never able to conceive a baby with Jack. It was heartbreaking at the time, but in the end, it was a small miracle. When the relationship had finally worn itself out, I was able to just walk out the door. No kids to think about, no house to fight over. I was one of the lucky ones. So many of my friends are stuck in bad marriages because of kids or money. I had neither, and probably never will. It is then that I realize Georgia is probably never leaving. Her decision to procreate is a tar enveloping her. She is stuck.

"Georgia, I'm happy for you," I say.

She looks up from her glass; her green eyes are liquid. "Really?"

"Yes. If you want another baby, then that's wonderful. You should have another baby," I say. I don't mean it, but it's what she needs to hear. I want to rescue her, to pull her from the clutches of the status quo. She deserves better. In that moment I realize just how much we have in common. A year ago, I *was* her. My family and my friends had to stand back and watch as Jack and my weight pulled me into a pile of quicksand that threatened to engulf me. Now, I feel loose and free, my body is less, my commitments are less. Yet, my life now is so much more.

"Are you okay?" Georgia's voice is drowned out by a mariachi band springing to life in the distance.

"Yes, I'm fine," I say, and I suddenly realize the conversation has shifted. We're not talking about her unhappy marriage anymore. We're talking about my unproductive uterus.

Because of my inability to have children, Georgia always asks if I'm okay after she talks about her son or anything baby related, like my infertility is a an eggshell around me that she is always afraid of cracking. And there was a time when that was probably true. I used to cry myself to sleep at night at the thought of other women's hips widening, breasts lactating, and bellies rounding. I used to avoid baby showers, baby stores, and anything that would remind me of the barren tomb inside of me.

"You know, the doctors didn't say you would never be able to have one," Georgia whispers loudly as she leans in towards me. An overeager waiter interrupts us five more times to see if we'd like some more chips, another drink, some queso blanco, a back rub, our cars washed. I know he's eyeing up Georgia.

"Georgia," I say when the annoying boy has slipped out of sight, "that time in my life is over. I blew it. I'm getting too old to start all over again."

I'm only twenty-eight, but time is growing thin in my mind. Ten years ago, when I first made the decision to love Jack and to build a life with him, time was thick and stubborn, and I thought he'd be there forever. Now, he's running away from me, slipping through my fingers. I'm only twenty-eight, yet I don't yet see how absolutely ridiculous my statement is.

"I'm really happy for you Georgia," I say, and maybe I do mean it.

"Are you sure?"

"Yes," I repeat as the waiter lowers steaming plates of food in front of us. *No, we don't need another drink yet. No, we don't want more chips. No, you can't braid my hair. Jesus Christ this guy is annoying.*

"Well, we're gonna try. We'll see what happens," she says.

I smile, and as we eat our food, I realize that I shouldn't be so quick to slide down her straw and assume her fertility. Having another baby with a man she does not love will be yet another string wrapping itself around them, tethering her to unhappiness. For the first time in my life, I am string-free. And I think I may want to enjoy that for a while.

Georgia's body is like a well oiled machine. She tries for a baby, and she gets one. Twenty-eight days after her announcement at the Mexican restaurant, she is pregnant.

Chapter Thirty-One

I am at my desk on a Friday afternoon when I get the call. "Hi. It's me."

"Hi you." My insides recognize him immediately. The voice of my teenage boyfriend, the first boy I ever loved. Ollie. My pulse quickens.

"How are you?" he asks.

"I'm good," I say, and for the first time in months I mean it. This is the game we have always played. He calls, or I call, depending on who is the more lonely of the two. We talk, we reconnect, we laugh, and we hang up. Then, months slip away like pages flipping in a book, sometimes years, and we do it all over again. Ollie once said that sometimes he just needs to make sure there is someone in the world who still loves him. *There will always be someone*, I told him.

"How's life?" he asks over the hum of power tools behind him. He is a mechanic at a small garage in Scranton. He has been working there for the past five years. Before that, he worked at a brake place. Before that, he attempted to open his own garage, but picked the wrong partner and everything went downhill fast. Ollie is like my Polaris, my North Star. I know where he is at all times.

"I'm divorced," I say. I don't know why, but I feel like it's crucial to the conversation. Throughout this cat and mouse we play, I have always had the tether of marriage preventing me from staying on the phone long enough to hear Ollie whisper those words: *I want to see you*. The same phrase he would utter into my fifteen-year-old ears that would cause me to go running to him with my arms and legs spread wide open.

"Oh, I'm sorry. What happened?"

"I…I…" Suddenly, even I don't really know what happened, and I realize I haven't even thought about it in weeks. How would I explain it? We met when we were sixteen, seventeen years old, we fell madly in love. We started to depend on one another, lean on one another. But as we grew up, we started to resent one another. We became entangled in a web of fear and need. I became a bitter, angry woman. He became a prisoner of his own addictions. Then, one day, he leaned so much that I eventually toppled over. Then, Sarah came along and saved us both. "We just grew apart," I finally say.

"Aww, I'm sorry," Ollie says.

"No, don't be, really. It's a really good thing," I tell him.

Silence.

"I want to see you," he says in a low voice.

I don't know why I agreed to meet him. The best explanation I can offer is that I was still making some bad decisions. While I was growing stronger each day, there was still a vat of jelly in the center of me when it came to boys. Ollie, in particular. But something told me to go. Some invisible force pulling me to him. Maybe it was stupid, or maybe, it was fate.

When I do see him, hours later at a small North Scranton sports bar, it is as if the last ten years crumble to dust between us. He is just as I left him. Small, confident, and powerful. He is shocked by my weight loss, a fact I forgot to mention on the phone earlier. *You look wonderful*, he says as he looks me up and down and his eyes light up like fireworks. Our past is complicated, he has hurt me tremendously in my life, a fact that my stomach will not let me forget, flipping and shaking in his presence. But he has loved me, too. A fact that my heart will not allow me to overlook. We talk briefly about our lives until a five-piece band starts humming and vibrating in the corner of the room. We stand at a tall table, two mugs of Miller Lite and a million unspoken words between us.

Ollie is music. He's the Eagle's "Wasted Time", Ozzy Osborne's "Goodbye to Romance", Peter Gabriel's "In Your Eyes." He's every sad song that has ever crossed my ears. Every sorrowful lyric that has ever crossed my lips. So, it seems fitting that the band seems to be on a strict diet of melancholy.

"Oh, I love this song," I lean across the table and whisper into his ear as a red-haired woman starts singing a rather flat rendition of Fleetwood Mac's "Silver Springs." I move closer to Ollie. His hand slides up and down my back. His eyes are like crescent moons hanging low in the sky, gazing at me. This is what I love about him. The way he looks at me. Like I'm fifteen again, just waiting for him to leave his mark on me in some way. I should run the other way, but I don't. I can't. His eyes on me in that moment are everything. It's as if time has been frozen. His hand slips down around my waist now, and he pulls my hip into his. We are the same height and the same width. We stand with his arm casually connecting us and our jeans rubbing together so intensely that I'm sure I can smell smoke.

Then, as the music slips from our ears, Ollie lets go and moves away. "Timmy's going to meet us here," he says while the band is discussing their next song.

"Oh great! I just ran into him a few months ago," I say, slightly disappointed that Ollie's best friend will be crashing our reunion.

"Really? He didn't mention that." Ollie's lips suck down the last of his beer.

"Do you want another? I'll buy." I grab his empty mug.

Minutes later, as I carry two mugs of beer to our tall table, I see Timmy has planted himself in my spot. He is tall and thin, and he towers over both Ollie and me. He greets me with a hug, he is familiar in a sense I have never felt before, like the only good parts of my past wrapping themselves around me.

The three of us close the bar, laughing, reminiscing, and sinking down beer after beer. I hold onto my caps, each one a reminder of the points I am consuming. Each beer is two points. I'm out of practice with my drinking and by the time I have seven caps in my hand, I can no longer stand up straight. I begin to lean, first on Ollie, then on Timmy. They don't seem to mind.

The band leaves at one and we leave at two. It is a long drive back to Wilkes-Barre, so Ollie offers to let me stay at his house. For a moment, as we stand under the street light, deciding how I will get home, I see Timmy turn to me with what I think is genuine concern. I imagine Jennie, Georgia, Pantsuit Pam, and Stephanie telling me not to leave with Ollie, their voices twirling in my head like ribbons of reason. But they are no match for the fifteen-year-old version of myself, and that's who I am when I am with Ollie.

"Okay, let's go," I slur and slip into the passenger seat of my own car.

The next morning, it is the familiar tango of disappointment and self-loathing. Even though Ollie and I passed out cold, with a million miles of space between us, I still let him know that I *would* have fallen right back into bed with him. I tipped my hand before the cards were even dealt.

"I'm such an asshole," I say into my cell phone as I'm making the forty-minute drive home. "All that fucking progress and I'm going to blow everything on Ollie." My voice is scratchy from the pack of cigarettes I smoked last night. The air is hazy and it sticks to my windshield as I drive, completely distracted and on the phone, down Interstate 81.

"No you're not," Georgia assures me, "You're just human. You had a slip, it's no big deal."

"And it's *Ollie*," I remind her.

"Yes, and it's Ollie."

Chapter Thirty-Two

"What did you want to be when you were young?" Pantsuit Pam asks as she clicks around us like a lioness circling her cubs. "Think about yourselves at five or six years old. What did your future look like to you?"

It's Thursday night, six nights after my reunion with Ollie, and the shame of that decision is still lingering around me like a fog. Pam stands unusually close to me and for a minute I worry that she can see through the film engulfing me.

"How many of you have achieved your dreams, and how many of you have let your weight stand in the way?" No one in the room raises their hand. Instead, a low murmur of grief can be heard snaking its way around us. Pantsuit Pam's instructions transport us into a world we haven't thought about in years, maybe even decades. As we sit in front of her, overweight, many of us unhappily married, many of us stuck in jobs we hate (with the exception of Bridget, a fashion buyer for Macy's who does nothing but talk about how much she loves her job every day, and wears enough makeup to single-handedly keep the cosmetic counter in business), it's quite clear we have drifted dramatically far from our originally-intended path.

No one ever says they want to grow up to be fat. Fat is a place you get stuck, like the Lincoln Tunnel at five o'clock on a Friday afternoon. Fat is a place where boys don't like you and other girls laugh at you. Fat is your cousin's First Holy Communion party, school on a warm June day, or a coworker's wedding. It's the last place you want to be. And when you end up there, you still have no idea how it happened. Because it wasn't supposed to be this way. You weren't supposed to be the fat girl.

When I was six, I wanted to grow up to be a ballet-dancing, baseball-playing mother. It's written in my baby book, scribbled in the soft cursive of my mother's hand. These three things seemed attainable to me at six years old; within reach, feasible. But by the time I began the pursuit of these careers, I was already chunky in places where others were slim. In ballet, I was clumsy and uncoordinated. In baseball, on a little league team, I fared no better–scared off by seeing a teammate's nose broken by a fast pitch.

But all was not lost. On my list of dreams, I still had my last and final choice: *mother*. The label that would elude me for years to come. But at six years old, there was never any doubt in my mind that I would grow up to have children of my own someday. As a teenager, I was a natural babysitter. As a young adult, I stepped into a maternal role with Jack's little sisters, mostly out of necessity, but also out of love. It wasn't until I was told that having children would be difficult, maybe impossible, that the air drained from that dream like a balloon with a slow leak.

Still, if you drilled down into the core of me, you would find it: small shards of that wish still in existence, pieces that have survived through the high tide of disappointment, the mountains of failed pregnancy tests, and the tears shed over each. Motherhood was like a loved one on life support; I knew I had to let her drift away from me, but I just couldn't.

After the meeting, I sit in my car for a long while and think. It's time to come clean, to be honest with myself. This life I have created around me, this home inside of myself, is wonderful and interesting. I have friends, I have interests, and I have a sense of self that I had never really owned before. But there is something missing. Some foundation that has never been constructed. It's as if this life is floating, and there is nothing to anchor it to the ground. And then it occurs to me. I still believe, somewhere down deep, that I will fall in love and have babies. It's as if I am renting this life, just waiting for my real one–the one with babies and a good man and a fulfilling career–to come along.

Later that night as I sit in the middle of their apartment, I realize it is Heather and Sergio who have helped me realize this truth. I want what they have. They are a visual representation of what I'm working towards. Their adoration for one another is heartwarming. They move together like one being. They glow. I want to hug them, to run to them and envelop them in a potentially life-threatening embrace; the only problem is, the cake they served me for dessert was packed so ferociously with hash that I'm sinking into this bean bag chair and cannot find my way out.

Heather and Sergio have almost no furniture, and what they do have is either cheap, disposable, or belongs in the 1970s. Heather sits cross-legged on the floor cooing at baby Alto, while Sergio strums his guitar. They stare at one another with a calm, deep intensity. It's romantic, the thought of them having nothing, only each other. The room spins around me slowly, like a carousel with no music.

"Did Sergio tell you our news?" Heather's voice floats like a purple ribbon across the sky and into my ears.

"What?" I want to see it again, the ribbon.

"Did Serge tell you our news?" she yells.

I say nothing. Her words dance above me, tangling with Sergio's classical notes.

"We're moving to the west coast next month," Sergio says, ignoring me ignoring him.

"Oh yeah? For what?" I ask. My mouth is like the desert.

152

Sergio is like an eclipse. I can't seem to focus on him. He is electrified.

"I got a job with an organic farm," Heather says.

"You're leaving?" I ask. My heart sinks. My body feels heavy and for a minute a panic shoots through my blood. I imagine I'm fat again. I imagine the pounds I've shed crawling across the floor with beady red eyes. They are chanting and reaching out for me, trying to reattach themselves.

"Yes," Sergio mutters. Before I can react, a rotary phone rings in the kitchen. A phone still connected to a cord. A phone still connected to a *wall*.

"Sergio, can you come in here please?" Heather asks as she paces the avocado green linoleum in her bare feet. Her blonde hair is tied in a knot at the base of her neck and her ponytail is long and hangs over one shoulder like a noose. She holds the phone with one hand and bites the fingernails on the other. Rainbows shoot from her lips. She is coral. She is earth. I am stoned.

An hour earlier, when Sergio invited me up to their apartment for dinner, he said in a whisper, "We have some cake."

"I can't eat cake," I answered loudly.

"No, silly, I mean cake. You know caaaake." His blue eyes spun in circles as the subtext he was working diligently to convey was barely glancing my forehead.

"Caaake?" My voice jutted up at the end like a fishing pole with a sudden bite.

"Amye. Hash cake." (A Gazillion Points)

"Oh. I've never done it. I don't know how I'll react," I confessed/warned him.

"You'll be fine."

And I am fine. He was right. I'm better than fine. I'm goddamned good. I could run that marathon I've always wanted to run, right now. All 26.2 miles of it. I could swim across Lake Wallenpaupack, climb a mountain, or dance the Rumba, if only I could get out of this fucking beanbag that is melting under me like a hot marshmallow. I'm usually not the first one in line to get high, but hash packed into a cake? That's something I can get behind.

"Sergio?" Heather yells into the living room. "I need you!"

Before the words slip from her lips Sergio is on his feet and throwing Alto onto my body.

"Here," he says, "Hang onto him a sec, will ya?"

I slide to a sitting position and cradle the baby in my arms. I hold him like Heather holds him, like he is mine, like I have held a million babies before and he makes one million and one. His eyes are little stars poking out at me from a universe so expansive it threatens to engulf the entire room. His lips are velvet and his hair is sugar. He is the most content human being I have ever seen. His little stars look up at me and he smiles. His blond head nestles into the crook of my left arm.

"The baby likes you," Heather says reappearing in the doorway.

In that moment, a cauldron deep down inside of me boils over. I am a collision of warmth and want. I am supposed to do this. *This*, right here. If Pantsuit Pam were here right now, I would pull back the curtain between us and reveal this moment as my answer to her riddle. This, is what I always wanted my life to be: a baby in my arms. Somehow, someway, this is what I have been waiting for my entire life. All of it: the weight loss, the shedding of Jack, all of the pain and anguish has been for *something*…this something. Suddenly, a once-deflated dream becomes inflated. *This* becomes a new possibility. Holding Alto is like holding the sun, and in his rays, the news of losing my friends is somehow lessened.

Chapter Thirty-Three

I have somehow deluded myself into thinking that Ollie and I can have a normal friendship; That I can smile and pretend he didn't destroy my formative years or bash my self-esteem to death with a rock. I should know better. I am almost thirty years old. I should know by now that Ollie and I only work on two speeds, love and hate, and we never seem to be able to coast comfortably between them. Still, I fool myself into thinking that I am now residing in that coveted grey area.

That gray area looks like this: Ollie, Timmy, and myself sitting around Ollie's living room two to three nights a week, getting stoned, sipping beer, and talking about what we want to do with our lives. I strum on my guitar while Timmy attempts to sing. He loves the way I play, and makes me go through every song in my repertoire. I'm amazed that he can identify every Indigo Girls song by its opening chord progression. Ollie pokes fun at us, and we all hold our stomachs, laugh, and roll like marbles on the floor.

But it's not just sitting around getting tipsy. Together, the three of us have intense conversations that cause us to examine our lives in a new way. One night, Timmy suggests writing our worst fears on a slip of paper and burning them in the fireplace. After much pot, this seems like a brilliant idea, and Ollie lights the gas insert, despite the late-summer heat hanging over the trailer park like cotton. Ollie writes that no one will ever understand him. I want to punch him in the face. *Do you know how many years I have spent trying to understand you? Turning myself inside out for you? No one fucking understands you because you won't let them.* Instead, I smile, and nod.

Timmy's fear is that his father will never be proud of him. I ask, *can we write more than one?* Finally, I decide to write the worst thing I can think of: that no one will ever see the real me. Then, like little flags of surrender, the slips of paper wave to us as the orange flames suck them into the inferno.

Nights always end the same way. All of us crawling into our respective sleeping places, Ollie and I miles apart in the bed and Timmy on the couch. But I can never sleep, and within minutes I stumble back out into the living room where Timmy and I sit and talk until the sun begins to creep through the poorly sealed trailer door. We talk about everything we've ever done, wanted, cared for, and lost. We are like teenagers, engulfing one another's ideas and dreams with a ravenous appetite. I talk a lot about Jack, about the divorce and what has come after. I don't realize it at the time, but Timmy is helping me heal. He's listening, intensely. He's massaging the darkness from my core, and replacing it with a lightness.

Things go on like this for a few weeks. We drink, we smoke, and we heal. Everything is fine. Then, it isn't. Having been invited for dinner, I walk through the door with my overnight bag in one hand and my guitar strapped across my shoulder. Ollie is standing at the kitchen counter on the phone. I sneak over to him, kiss his cheek, and begin making myself comfortable. His phone call is vague. There's androgynous pronouns, a lack of substance, and a fog over the details.

"I have to go somewhere for a little bit," he announces after he clicks his phone closed.

"Where? What about dinner?"

"I'll be back, I just have to run an errand."

"Okay, I'll wait here," I say.

Ollie is gone for a long time. The hours tick off the clock, the sun sets and the stars rise. I call his cell and he doesn't answer. When Timmy shows up, I share my concern. He suggests we go for a ride, *maybe when we get back, Ollie will be here.* I agree, and we end up drinking a few beers and off-roading through the woods in his beat-up Chevy Blazer. I've never been off-roading in my life, but pretend to be calm and cool as I bounce from my seat and thin branches snap and scratch the windows. At a clearing, we find some teenagers drinking around a bonfire and park about fifty feet from them. I slug more and more beer, not even noticing that I've started to slur. Timmy opens the back of his truck and we sit on the tailgate, his feet scraping the dry dirt under us, mine swinging six inches off the ground through the dense night air. We spend a long time looking at the stars which spread out over us like white sand against a black sky.

"Do you realize that no one ever really looks up?" Timmy

156

whispers.

"That's true," I answer. With that statement he has articulated a sense of relief inside of me, and I realize that I am finally looking up, for the first time in a long, dark year.

Minutes later, I wander off to bum a cigarette from one of the teenagers, and I suddenly notice that the bonfire is actually a stack of burning tires. *What are you guys, fucking crazy?* I slur. Timmy and I laugh so hard that I bend over in pain from my sides hurting, and as I come up for air, he kisses my cheek softly. A brush of his lips against my skin and I feel goose bumps forming on my arms.

When we return to Ollie's house, there is a foreign car in the driveway.

"Oh shit, Kerri's here," Timmy blurts out.

"Who's Kerri?" I ask. I'm so clueless that I actually search my memory banks for Ollie's sister's name. *Marie, no Renee. Not Kerri.*

"Oh. She's a girl Ollie's been sort of seeing," Timmy answers as he climbs from the truck.

I slide from the passenger seat like silly putty. "What do you mean? Like a girlfriend?"

"Yeah, sort of. Ollie hasn't mentioned her?"

"Um, no," I whisper. I don't know why I care or why a fuse lights in my belly, but it does. Maybe it's a learned response to the pain that is so familiar between Ollie and me. I am so full of blind rage that I can barely walk.

"I thought it was strange that you were sticking around. Listen, just act like you're with me, okay?" Timmy says and slides his long, thin arm around my back.

Kerri, a petite blonde, is sitting on Ollie's couch wrapped in his arms. She's cute and little. I imagine I could fold her up and stick her in my purse. Without saying a word, I march past them, looking for my bag. Timmy follows me down the narrow hallway into Ollie's bedroom.

"What are you doing?" he asks.

"What does it look like? I'm leaving," I say in a rush of anger.

I'm beyond pissed, but I can't really articulate why. My hands shake as I shove my toothbrush back into its small Ziploc bag.

"Wait, Amye, don't go. Come on," Timmy's voice is like a velvet rope from his soft lips, wrapping itself around me. I want to stay, with Timmy, but I know I can't. I cannot let another man make a fool of me. No way. I stomp back through the living room, grab my bag from behind Ollie's couch, and leave. I say nothing as I walk out, slamming the cheap trailer door behind me. My shoes kick up pebbles as I cross the dirt driveway to my small Saturn. As I climb in, I hear the trailer door slam again. And in a moment Timmy is running towards me.

"I'm leaving, Tim, don't try to stop me," I yell to him as I start the engine. A small exhaust leak makes my car sound more like a motorcycle.

"Amye, don't go, please."

"Do you have any idea how many times that man has hurt me in my life?" I ask. It's the same scene all over again, Ollie fucking everything up and Timmy trying to smooth things over on his behalf. It's as if I'm watching a movie of my life and I've rewound all the way back to the beginning. "There's nothing you can say for him, Tim, I'm leaving. I'm not fifteen years old anymore."

Timmy walks closer, resting his hand on my half-open car door. "I'm not asking for Ollie. I'm asking for me."

I look up at his face. His hazel eyes are calm.

"I just, I don't want you to go," he stares right at me. "I am a better person when you are around." His words hang between us like white noise, everything else fades away. "I'm begging you, take a walk with me, take a drive with me, I don't care what we do, just stay. Stay with *me*."

"I can't. I have to go." I pull my car door from his grip and leave. In the rearview mirror he becomes a man shrinking to a boy, then he is gone.

I call Georgia on the ride home. "Ollie has fucked me over again," I tell her.

"Oh, Amye, I'm sorry," she prepares herself for the explosion of emotion sure to follow this statement. The statement that, by now, must sound like an echo.

"You know what? It's actually okay," I tell her, "I'm okay with it."

"You are?"

"Yep. And in other news, I think Timmy likes me."

And just like that, my decade-long obsession with Ollie comes to an end. Ollie and I will eventually come to know one another as friends, but it will take a long road, a long while, and much water under the bridge between us. For now, this new life of mine is filled to the brim with people who love me, and Ollie doesn't. Plain and simple.

Chapter Thirty-Four

Sheer boredom has placed me back at one of Smithy's shows. Hours earlier, Joe called and asked if I'd like to drive down to Hazleton and hear Smithy open for a bigger, more prominent local band. I struggled at first. While we still work together, and have seen one another countless times in that environment, I have yet to see Smithy on stage since the last time we ended up in bed together. I wasn't sure I had enough distance to resist the magnetic force pulling me to the front of the crowd, the compulsion to act like a desperate groupie. But I couldn't hide forever. I curled my hair, lined my lips, threw on a knee-length skirt, and headed for Hazleton.

The bar is somewhere I've been before. It's mostly known for "Penny Till You Pee." A gimmick in which the bar managers seal off the restrooms with yellow construction-strength tape, drop the price of their cheapest beer to a penny for a draft, and wait until someone breaks the man-made barrier. Once the tape is broken, the drafts are back up to a dollar, or whatever they were previously. This sounds great, and Georgia and I have taken great advantage of this in the past, ordering nine or ten beers at once, ensuring we would drink cheap for the rest of the night. But recently, the event has led to some trouble in the neighborhood. It seems that in an effort to avoid breaking the bathroom seal, some men and women had taken to propping open the fire doors at the back of the club and relieving themselves outside. Turns out the neighbors were unhappy with the urine content of their lawns and complained to the police. Soon, the club managers started padlocking the fire doors, resulting in a short life for the yellow tape.

Tonight, however, drafts are regular price in anticipation of the crowd that will be drawn here not by Smithy's band, but by another group that has been gaining in popularity across the area. It is Labor Day weekend, and the bars and clubs in Northeast Pennsylvania are usually packed full of young people who make a lot of disposable income and bad decisions. Joe and I part ways the minute we push through the dark gray doors. He has promised that he will be my rock, my go-to, in case the presence of Smithy is too much and I feel that familiar pull. But almost immediately, Joe spots a cute red-head at one of the tall, circle-shaped tables in the bar, and leaves me to fend for myself.

We're late, and the band has started already. The main lights are low, leaving a few light bulbs of varying colors hanging low over the stage. The bass is deep and inviting, a murmur in Smithy's hands. His bald, shiny head is red, green, blue, as he moves through the rainbow illuminating the stage which is nothing fancy, merely a riser constructed of cheap plywood that bends with every hop and jump by the singer. The crowd is thin, a few girls bopping up and down with glistening beer bottles in their hands, some guys standing off to the sides, discussing which of the girls will be their next conquest. Smithy spots me, and with a familiar head bob, he invites me to his side of the lifter. I stand in front of him, our eyes almost level, and sway my hips slightly as the next few songs ping pong around the growing crowd. He's giving me that look. The one where his tongue slips slightly from his lips, his head tilts low, but

160

his eyes stay on me. This is the signal, the announcement of after-show festivities.

Six months ago, my heart would pound right out of my chest when I saw this look. Tonight, however, I have other things on my mind. It's that kiss. That soft, gentle, brush of a kiss that Timmy so carefully placed on my cheek as stars the size of marbles collected over our heads. A tiny shiver slides up my back when I remember the smell of him so close to me. I can see his eyes spring to life when I talk about politics and his hands animated in the air as he rants about the 2000 election. I can picture his smile as he watches me play the Indigo Girls on my guitar. I hear him over and over again asking me not to drive away, then I see him vanishing behind me as I drove. Suddenly, I want him in a way I never have before. I wave to Smithy and make my way to Joe, who by this time is sitting on an uneven barstool with the redhead on his lap.

"I'm leaving. Can you find your own way home?" I yell over the pounding beat of the drums.

"Um." Joe looks at his new-found friend and she smiles back. "Yeah, I'll be fine," he says.

Across the club, Smithy looks puzzled. He spots me near the doors and bobs his head once again. I shrug my shoulders, turn, and push the doors out into the crisp September night. The music is muffled as I walk across the parking lot, but I can hear Radiohead's Creep, the baseline like a snake trying to pull me back. He's playing my song.

I call Timmy immediately from the car. *I can't stop thinking about you*, I say. *I'll be right there*, he answers. That night, he drives to my apartment and we talk until four o'clock in the morning, and when the conversation winds down, we climb into my bed. With Timmy, sex is different. It's not drunk, sloppy, or desperate. There's choreography to our movements, a ballet between us. We glide over one another with precision and care. We fit together like finely-matched dancers. Under the cover of darkness he speaks Spanish in my ear as he navigates the folds of my body. His hands are large

161

and strong, his skin is like milk. His voice is a lake I could slip into.

When we wake the next morning, our fingers are still intertwined. There is no regret hanging between us. I am calm and content. There is no leap to desperation, no dreams of a future with this man. There is just a stillness. We wrap our arms around one another and lie on my bed until the sun is hot and bright. My head is nestled in the crook of his arm, my nose against his neck. I breathe him in.

"I see you," he whispers.

"I know."

And outside of my window, the whole world falls away.

Chapter Thirty-Five

When I was young and still protected by the web of security my parents had woven over me, the worst thing in the world I could imagine was to be left. If my mother and father dropped us with my grandmother for an evening, I sobbed until they reluctantly returned. When my father went to work in the morning, I cried and cried, and cried, until he came home. I stomped extra hard on the floors of our six-unit apartment building, and blasted Billy Joel's *Glass Houses* on my boom box with the speakers to the floor, in hopes that complaints from our downstairs neighbors would reel my father back to us.

Once, in a convenience store, my mother wandered into the next aisle, just out of my line of sight. I panicked, screamed, and carried on like I was being sucked into a vacuum until she reappeared, red-faced and apologetic to the onlookers. I hated being left, and that quirk, that defect, translated into adulthood as a fear of abandonment. It kept me grasping to things that were unhealthy, just because it was better to have something than nothing.

Now, watching my friends, Sergio and Heather, pack their "furniture" into a small U-Haul truck on a Saturday morning in

September, I have to fight the urge to scream again like I did in that store, in hopes that my wails will pin them to my chest. But I can't, I won't. They are due to be at the organic farm in Monterey, California, by mid week, and they have a whole country to zig zag across. I am letting them go. I sit on the back steps of our building bouncing Alto on my lap as the two of them carry everything they own past me.

I know in that moment that I am losing something valuable. And that even though we have promised that we will write, visit, dream, think often of each other, I will probably never see them again. They are drifters. They move and move and move, and never let their roots sink down into the earth's crust. They never stay long enough to fall in love with or betray another person. They are nomads, but they are nomads together. They represent all I wish I could be, carefree, rolling with the punches of life, floating through the world.

"Are you going to be okay?" Heather asks as they throw the last box into the half-empty truck.

"Yes. I'll be fine, don't worry," I tell her. I don't want her last thought of me to be that I will unspool like a roll of ribbon after they drive away. They have spent so much time with me. They have given me so much. They have helped me to write again, helped me to live with my decisions. They have helped shape my life.

"You'll keep writing won't you?" I'm not sure if she means creatively or writing letters to them, either way I will continue both.

"Yes," I say.

I hand Alto to Sergio and stand toe to toe with Heather. Tears well in her bright green eyes. Her hug is like an envelope that seals around me. It is warm and tight and full of emotion. Baby Alto is locked into his carrier and I kiss his forehead seven times before he is whisked away into the van. The September air is sweltering and this moment is covered in a hazy layer of sweat. Sergio starts the ignition, but hops out of the driver side for one last goodbye.

He puts his hands on my shoulders and looks in my eyes.

"You're a smart girl. You have your shit together in a way that most people don't," he says to me.

"I love you," I tell him hard, like I want to stuff it inside of him.

"We love you. Keep building your life. It's really going to be something."

And like that, they go away from me, a trail of thin exhaust running behind them.

Later that day, as I'm walking down the street, I am suddenly stunned by how beautiful my surroundings are. South Franklin Street is right in the historic part of Wilkes-Barre, and is lined with Victorian houses and Gothic buildings. Cherry blossom trees drape their arms over the sidewalk and cover everything with a beautiful film. It's like everything around me is working overtime to prove its viability, like I am noticing it all for the first time.

My thoughts drift to my friends, their whole life in a van, carving a path across the landscape. I regret not asking them to stay. But I know they needed to leave, to explore, to be free to roam the world together. I'm starting to realize that people slip in and slip out of your life and that there is only one constant, unchanged, stationary object: you. I have lost everything that I once depended on, and I survived. Maybe I'm not that same kid who clung irrationally to her mother, or held on to things and people too tight. Maybe, just maybe, I'm starting to grow up.

Chapter Thirty-Six

I imagined it would feel differently, the transition into couple-hood. After all, I had been raised on a steady diet of soap operas and those stories are what comprise the base of me. Since the age of five, I have been following *the Guiding Light, As the World Turns, The Young and The Restless,* and *The Bold and the Beautiful,* religiously. I have witnessed wives driving off bridges, baby thefts, spiked drinks, espionage, acquaintance rape, kidnappings, identity switching, tampered paternity tests, demonic possession, evil twins, interrupted weddings, and even pregnancy by turkey baster. It's no wonder, with these seeds planted deep in my subconscious, that my ideas of love and how the heart works have been skewed from the beginning.

Watching soap operas is a ritual steeped in tradition in my family. My mother was a stay-at-home mom, and she and I watched her stories every day. Thirty years earlier, she and my grandmother did the same. It was a maternal yarn that tied us to one another. The Bauers, the Lewises, the Newmans, and the Spauldings have been in my life for as long as I can remember. I know their family histories, the bends in their family trees, their fights and grievances, better than I know my own.

At one point, in college, while I was still searching for a possible career, a dream to chase, it seemed natural to drift towards what I knew best. I lived for my soap operas, and I decided I wanted to become a network writer. I branched out, began taping all three channels worth, ten soap operas a day. At night, I watched them all and worked on amateur scripts. Then, as the industry began to die a slow death, I gave up that dream and turned to the way less lucrative: poetry. But those story-lines and characters flow through my blood. You see, beneath the surface of my writing and my perception of all things, runs a river of melodrama and intrigue so swift and strong that sometimes it's difficult to keep that river within her banks.

So, when Timmy and I begin to fall into something deeper than friendship, a puddle muddled with more than just lust and sex, I am caught unaware by the lack of pageantry. Our move into relationship status is surprisingly unadorned and plain. I had imagined bells and whistles, fire and heat, the kind of burning that makes you want to jump out of your skin and into an ice bath. The rush of passion that I had watched played out on the small screen every day: men working to win the women they loved, five-piece orchestras, rugs lined with rose pedals, skimpy lingerie, last-minute trips to the Italian coast, a monumental wooing process that always won the woman's heart in the end. I imagined my first real relationship would be similar.

Instead, our actions are calm and rational. We are lying in one another's arms, laughing at some stupid joke one of us has made. The morning is soft and surrounds us with light.

"I think we have something here," one of us says.

"Yes, I think we do," the other one answers.

I can't remember how it starts, I only remember how it ends. Hours have slipped away somewhere and it grows dark outside. Timmy is making phone calls. He has been dating a few girls, nothing serious, but enough intimacy has passed between them that he feels he owes them a courtesy call. He tells them all, Karen, Alicia, Big Bird, I can't recall their names, that he is going to be unavailable in the near future. He tells them, with a slight sense of euphoria in his voice, that he has found someone great. He has found who he believes to be his soul mate. And he's talking about me! I pretend that I have to make calls of my own. *Oh yes*, I say, *I have to call so and so and break their heart into a million pieces with the news that I am off the market.* Instead, I sneak into the bathroom and call Georgia first, then Jennie. There is no one waiting for me on the other side of coupled.

Later, when I hear Timmy on the phone again, this time with his father, he uses the word girlfriend for the first time. The word floats into my brain and I want to cry at the untainted beauty of its meaning. I want to hold it in my mouth, press it against my cheek, and protect it from the world. *Girlfriend.* It's such a simple and easy label. No complications barnacled to its side. No bad memories holding it underwater to drown. It is pure and good.

That is how our life together begins. In a school house, on an ordinary day, as a tenuous agreement between two willing parties to forge forward into a relationship. There are no soap opera style dramatics, no jealous flare-ups, no ex-lovers coming back from the dead, no unwanted babies, no Machiavellian schemes, and no fires to put out. This new relationship is unlike anything I have ever known. It is measured and calm, like a dam, a system of locks and levees designed to keep that river of melodrama inside of me from reaching her flood stage.

Chapter Thirty-Seven

My grandmother dies the day before my birthday. It's early morning and I'm lying in bed, flirting with the snooze button, when I get the call. Timmy is by my side, stretched out like he belongs in my bed. Our relationship is only days old, still in its infancy, still wearing her new car smell. The night before, Joe, Aaron, and even Smithy all showed up to have a few drinks and push me one year closer to thirty. Sergio and Heather sent a birthday card from somewhere in the California desert. *All is well, miss you like hell*, was all it said, with a smiley face drawn underneath.

"My grandmother is dead," I say.

"I'm sorry," Timmy whispers. His voice is lost in the thick pillow.

"Me too."

I have never had anyone I cared about die before. I never really knew either of my grandfathers—my mother's father was dead before I was a year old, and my father's father kept himself at arm's length from all of us for most of my life. But my grandmother was different. I grew up with her. Jennie and I slept at her house almost every weekend. We watched *Solid Gold* on her small color television, she dragged us to church every Sunday, and we drowned ourselves in buckets of her costume jewelry. My parents were very young when they had Jennie, and still pretty young when I came along, so we were unusually close to both of our grandmothers, who in a sense, helped raise us. Losing one of them was like losing a tether to my childhood.

The days that follow are a blur. My father is calm and quiet. In shock. Orphaned and alone. My heart aches for him. He feels guilt

167

and shame. He second guesses every decision he made in the past year: plucking his mother from her home, setting her up in the nursing home, and visiting her every other day, instead of every day. His instinct to protect her from pain had been learned behavior—my grandfather was a drummer, he ran around on her, and my father was always there to pick up the pieces. But he couldn't protect her from the freight train of dementia that ripped through her body. And now, she is lost to us.

When Jennie came in from New York, we rode together, just the three of us, to the funeral home, where my father picked out the best fucking casket money could buy. It was nicer than my apartment.

There's food, lots of food. The doorbell rings every ten minutes like a pinball machine. People send lunch meat (2 points a slice) and chocolate éclairs (a million points). I can't eat anything. Neither can anyone else.

But there's a problem: my family is top-heavy with girls. My grandmother had two sons, my father and his brother. My father only had girls, and his brother only had one son. So there is a lack of men or boys to act as pallbearers. My cousin Kit will do it of course, and Josh can be counted on. Add three extraneous far away second-cousins and nephews, and my father still comes up short. "What about your friend Timmy?" my father asks me.

It's a hard question to pose to someone you've only been dating for a few weeks. In fact, I almost don't. There's no way in hell I ever would have dreamed of asking Jack, even if we were still married. He would be too nervous, too overcome with anxiety to even attend the funeral, let alone carry my grandmother to her final resting place. My grandmother's death would be something I would have had to suffer through alone, just like everything else.

"I have something to ask you, and please, feel free to say no. It's not a big deal," I say to Timmy on my cell phone. My whole family is still hunkered down around my father's house, and I barely manage to escape to the backyard for a smoke.

"What's up?"

"Well, we only have five pallbearers for the funeral and we need six. I was wondering if you'd be willing to help us." I hold my breath, certain that he will say no; he barely knows my family. Just having to ask him kills me. It's been a long time since I asked a man for something that really counted. This really counted.

"Absolutely, no problem!" Timmy doesn't even hesitate.

"Thank you so much," I say. I hang up, and despite all of the tragedy and sadness gathering around me, I smile. *What a good man*, I think. Something I haven't thought about any man, ever. Except for my father.

The funeral is sad and wonderful all at the same time. My grandmother was a very popular woman; valedictorian of her high school and still close to her childhood buddies. If you can measure a person's wealth by the friends they keep, she was a very rich woman. I have a picture of us–me, Jennie, my father and Doreen– from the morning of the funeral. We are standing on his front porch with our arms all intertwined. I am wearing a cute, short dress, one I would never have dared to wear before. The four of us are an ocean of black. Black shirts, black shoes, black clothes, black hair. But in the middle of all that darkness there is a smile, an ear to ear smile, plastered across my face.

Chapter Thirty-Eight

Alone, I am a star burning against the night sky. I am lost in a blanket of darkness, a heaving illuminated mass threatening to collapse in on itself. But together, Timmy and I are a galaxy, a vast wonderful world of possibilities. We are bright and organized, burning into one another with fire and fever. We are celestial. We are so fucking fantastic together that I know deep down inside, it is only a matter of time until we fizzle out, or at least until I fuck it all up.

Things have been going swimmingly thus far. Timmy has all

but moved in, staying six out of seven nights at my apartment. In the mornings, he crawls out of bed and makes coffee for the two of us. In the evenings, he sits and listens as I play my guitar. We talk constantly. We make love almost every day, in every nook and cranny of the apartment. We orbit one another in perfect harmony. But I am terrified. I have yet to tell Timmy about my addiction, about my daily uphill climb. I know I shouldn't be embarrassed, but I am. I'm ashamed that I am not strong enough to be thin on my own, that I need assistance.

Then, there's an element of insecurity. I know that if I just let myself, I could fall madly in love with this man. But I wonder if he could ever really fall in love with me. This thought is an aftershock from my divorce. This is what happens when someone leaves you for real. This is what breaks inside of you when someone walks out on you and earthquakes your foundation. When the person who is supposed to love you the most in the world, flips a switch and chooses another. And you are not enough, not *good* enough, anymore. That betrayal reverses something in your brain. It makes you doubt your market value. Because whether I ever want to admit it or not, there is a small sliver of truth to the idea that Jack left me because I let my body balloon into obesity.

And now, I cannot act like a normal, untainted, self-assured woman. Because I will never be that. You can carve every ounce of fat from my body, and I will still never be able to walk around naked in front of you, trust whole heartedly that you are where you say you are, or sleep at night basking in the calmness of our union. No matter how beautiful I look on the outside, I will always feel like I am selling you a used car that I know has been in an accident and will never again drive the same.

I wasn't supposed to be insecure anymore. Like swallowing a pill, losing weight was supposed to instantly fix all of these neurotic, self-conscious thoughts swelling inside my brain. But I'm beginning to realize that being fat for so long has created a gushing wound that may never truly heal.

"Take off your shirt," Timmy orders as we lie down together in our bed one fall night, cotton sheets and down-filled blankets enveloping us both.

"No," I whisper. With the lights still on this is not even in the realm of possibility.

"Take it off." Timmy's lips twist with determination. I lie beneath him, clinging to my white tank top.

"I can't."

"Why?" he asks.

Why? How do I explain away the ripples of extra skin hanging below my belly button like rings on a tree, only instead of telling of my past, they tell of the future, the potential for thick ankles and triple chins? How do I explain to someone who has never stepped foot in the land of heavy that the weight of belonging to such a place comes at the cost of sanity? Timmy has never been fat, in fact he has spent his entire life underweight. And that, right there, that fact is the vast expansive universe between us. My insistence on lights off during sex, my one too many "checking in" phone calls, or questions about late night bar visits, all combine to comprise the wormhole through which Timmy will have to plunge if he ever hopes to really understand me. A wormhole so vast in size and density that it would take someone solely dedicated to the cause to get through and survive. I don't know yet if Timmy has the resolve to hang in there. I hope he does, but I don't need him to. And that, right there, is the big difference in my life from a year ago. I don't *need* him to.

While I still cling to my shirt, a size medium that I stole from Jennie during a visit to Brooklyn, a clingy white cotton tank that maintains enough elasticity to shave an inch off my belly, Timmy quietly extends an arm and clicks off the lamp. And in the safety of the darkness we are once again stars in our galaxy, burning and bumping our way into one another's hearts, unsure of what will come next.

Chapter Thirty-Nine

When I was six, we moved a few blocks away from our apartment building into a new house. The house was nothing grandiose—a fixer-upper at best—but it was a place with a yard for Jennie and me to play, a driveway to park cars in, a garage to store our shit. It was what my parents had wanted for our family for so long, and we were all thrilled to live there. That is, everyone except for our cat, Tig.

Tig could not accept that we had moved, and every night like a breath inhaled in the darkness, Tig was sucked back to that place. He walked the six or seven blocks, slept on the porch of our old place, and then returned home for his breakfast each morning. We tried everything to get him to stay. If we locked the doors, Tig cried all night to get out. If we drove over there and brought him back, he just waited until the next night and left again.

My mother was beside herself. You see, she had rescued Tig, stolen him really, from another family in the apartment complex. They were a rowdy family of all boys and they were mean and abusive to Tig. My mother witnessed them hitting him, leaving him outside for days with no food, and then finally, tossing him off the second floor porch. My mother, having an enormous soft spot for animals, began feeding Tig, letting him into our apartment, and eventually throwing him into our car on moving day. So for her, this was personal. Tig was choosing abuse over my mother's gentle care, and she just couldn't quite wrap her brain around that.

But I, on the other hand, get it completely. It's that same reflex, that desire to return to what's comfortable, that has me circling the one place I never wanted to see again. For weeks now, I have been rogue, missing, hiding. I have been happily drowning in Timmy's love and acceptance, forgetting about points, calories, and grams of fiber. I've been masquerading as a normal girl. *Oh, sure I can go for wings tonight, and suck down six beers while I'm at it. Dessert? Sure, no problem. Movie popcorn with extra butter layered throughout? Yes, please! I'm normal. I can do these normal things.* Meanwhile, my scale has grown cold, crying and aching for my morning weigh in, the accountability, the reminder that I am not welcomed at the skinny's girls' table.

I hate that my life is this. A constant system of checks and balances. I hate that Timmy has to date someone who has to hold her beer can tabs in her pockets so she can track how many points she has kicked back, or that he has to wait while she searches the menu in a restaurant for something baked, skinless, and tasteless. So rather than explaining it all to him, I let myself go. I let my guard down, pretend my way into a zone of comfort that has never been good for me.

It's a calculated risk. Inside of me there is an addiction so strong, a monster that, once fed, could destroy me and everything I have worked so hard for. But I take that risk, and for the first few weeks, eight or nine maybe, of our relationship, Timmy knows me as a normal girl without a weight problem. A healthy, well-adjusted woman who is a little thick in the thighs, but is still easy on the eyes. I'm fun and carefree. I can hike, bike, and have sex in a variety of positions. It's easy. So much fucking easier this way.

Then, the day comes, like a scratchy silent movie. It's almost winter. The streets and sidewalks are stained white from the frost. The sun has set and it's only five o'clock. There in the middle of the nearly frozen landscape, my car coasts quietly around the concrete moat surrounding the Scranton McDonald's. There is my arm, extending from the car window and handing a young teenager a crumpled ten dollar bill. Next, I am parking in an isolated spot before turning off the engine. Then, the finale. Me, devouring a Quarter Pounder with Cheese like a cheetah feasting on a gazelle. Suddenly, I am like Tig, that old cat of ours. I am going home, I am returning to that which I once left. I am circling the drain, and at the bottom of that funnel is a lonely and dark place: a land where there is no Timmy, no babies waiting to be born, no good at all. I am being vacuumed back into a dark hole, and there's no guarantee that I'll have the strength to climb out *again.*

Chapter Forty

I am peeing behind a bush on Main Avenue in Wilkes-Barre when Timmy first says the words. The words every girls wants to hear. Except me.

"I love you," he blurts out. The phrase moves quickly and sneaks up on me like a mugger, sucking the air from my chest.

"Shut up!" I yell as I concentrate on my squatting. My dark urine pools into the crack of a sidewalk before heading downstream towards the flagpole.

We are on our way home from Murray's Bar, the same bar where I went on my first outing with Smithy almost a year earlier. Timmy and I stayed until closing. The house lights kicked on as we were still looped in one another's arms with our tongues tangled in a knot. Now, on the five block walk home to my apartment, the urge to pee has sent me hiding behind manicured foliage in front of the Wilkes-Barre Township Fire Department. I pull up my pants and rejoin Timmy. He is drunk and swaying in his stance.

"Why would you say such a thing?" I ask as we lean on one another like dominos.

"Because I do. I love you."

"I don't want you to," I say.

"Tough shit," he responds.

The night is thin and cool as we climb the stairs of the old schoolhouse together. Our laughter echoes off the high ceilings inside. Then, his hands are all over me and I barely get the door unlocked before we fall into a puddle of fused mouths and heavy breathing. Afterwards, we lie there on the floor, naked, staring at one another.

"I meant it you know," he starts.

"Don't. Don't say it," I order.

"Amye, please, listen to me. I love you."

"Come on," I say sitting up and searching for my top, "Let's go

174

to bed."

I have no real reason to distrust Timmy in any way. All of the evidence points to the fact that he does indeed *want* to be with me. He doesn't *need* to be with me. He is different from Jack in one major way: he's a grownup. He's lived on his own, he can take care of himself, and if I ever needed it, I have confidence that he could and would take care of me. He is honorable and worthy of my respect. My family loves him. But I still hesitate. I'm still scared.

Chapter Forty-One

Georgia suggests I may need some closure. And I'm starting to think she's right. The last contact I had with Jack was months ago, in a brief phone conversation laced with anger and guilt. Maybe I needed to talk to him, to find out why he stayed, and to get a few things off my chest as well. As it turns out, Jack works right around the corner, and when I call him up to meet for lunch the next day, he is cautious, but agreeable.

It is a Monday morning, and the city of Wilkes-Barre is coming to life after a long, cold weekend. The trees have started to lose their leaves, and a December wind is sending forgotten litter flying up and down the streets. I'm wearing jeans and a sweater, and stand with my arms wrapped around my chest as I wait outside of Jack's building for him to appear.

"Hey!" I hear him yell as he approaches me. He looks like shit. His hair is short and receding, his eyes are framed by droopy, purple circles, and his skin is the color of toothpaste. My stomach is calm and unaffected as we stand face to face.

"How are you?" I ask.

"Good, really good," he says loudly, and I recognize the nervous tremble in his words.

We have agreed to go to lunch, and while I would be just as happy walking to a local sandwich shop, Jack insists on showing me the used car he has just purchased. *You can't even pay for the one you*

175

have, and you bought a second???? I want to scream. I imagine my credit score dropping as we speak. But, I bite my tongue. It is not my fight anymore. I pull open my own door and slide onto the black leather seats.

Jack cannot stop talking, and drives the car fast and hard through the parking lot. As we approach the Market Street Bridge, the concrete structure that straddles the Susquehanna River, I grab my seatbelt and hold on for dear life. There is a panic in my stomach, and for one split second I fear he is going to drive us off the edge, plunging us to our deaths in the cold water. When we reach the other side, I am relieved.

Jack wants to eat at Wendy's, and I don't hesitate to agree. We both order our old "usual": double cheeseburgers with everything and a large order of fries. As I eat across from him, there is a familiarity that terrifies me. I remember this place, this life, this girl I once was. The top bun on my burger slides around and an orange glob of ketchup mixed with mustard falls onto my shirt. At first, I am terrified, wondering how I would explain this fast food stain to Pantsuit Pam, Timmy, or even worse, myself.

"Jack, I need to ask you something," I say as I shove a salty fry into my mouth.

"Shoot."

"Do you blame me for ruining your life?" I ask.

"Listen," he says as he lays his burger onto the foil placemat, "you were good to me, Aim, you were really good to me. It took me so long to realize that, but I have. And I'm sorry I took that for granted."

I have wanted to hear those words for so long that I press my back against the chair and let them wash over me. "Really?"

"Yes," he says.

"Jack, I want you to know that I never meant to hurt you. I'm so sorry I called you names and became so frustrated with your disease. I was very mean to you sometimes and you didn't deserve that," my regrets pour from my mouth like a waterfall. It feels good to be honest, with him and myself.

"It's fine. Like I said, I never realized how good I had it."

We talk for a whole hour. We rehash all of the major milestones in our relationship. Some of them good, most of them bad. The restaurant clears out around us, then fills up after a yellow bus pulls into the parking lot. We laugh as we remember the follies of our youth and the foolish dreams we shared. We tear up as we talk about the tender moments, the vulnerable spots inside each of us that will remain only ours forever. Our voices grow thin and tight as we touch on some of the topics we will never agree upon. I realize, sitting across from him again after so much has happened between us, that there is a very tiny piece of me that will always be solely his. We made something together, the two of us, something that no one will ever understand but us. Our life.

As we drive back over the bridge, my grip less intense on the seatbelt now, I feel okay with our past. *We did the best we could,* Jack says, *we were kids, that's all.* He loves Sarah, plans on asking her to marry him, and I'm happy for him. She does something for Jack that I never could. She treats him like an adult, lets him suffer the consequences of his own mistakes, something I never did. *I wish you all the happiness in the world, it's all I've ever wanted for you,* I tell him. And I truly mean it. What was once so passionate and hot between us has become cold and miles away.

I also know, now more than ever, what I need to do. I cannot go back to being this girl, the one who binges and retreats into the grip of her addiction. I need to come clean with everything, with everyone. If Timmy is going to be my partner, then I need to make sure he will be someone who understands that I climb uphill, over and over again, every single day. And he needs to support my sobriety, whole-heartedly. I need to go back to Pantsuit Pam, where I'm sure she will welcome me with open arms and no questions. I cannot go backwards, and never has that idea been so evident as it was today. Me, sitting in a fast food restaurant, gorging myself on calories while sitting across the table from Jack. I have two choices, *that* can be my life, or my life can be what it has been the past year, healthy and happy. I choose the latter.

Later that night, as Timmy and I lie in bed in the blackness of our apartment, his long, strong arm cradling my head, I become a faucet of vulnerability. The struggles with weight, the food addiction, the body image issues, all of it comes pouring out of me like water flowing over a dam. I tell him everything about the lunch with Jack, and even the return to the McDonald's parking lot. He says nothing, even his breath is still. And when I'm finished, I say the words I have felt swelling inside of me for months now.

"I love you," I whisper as tears stream down my cheeks.

And in that moment, with the raw brutality of my truth straddling us, we sleep fused together, connected.

The next morning, I wake up alone. At first, I imagine he has left, packed his bags and run off, scared of the fat girl with no self-control. Just as I am ready to sob like a crazy person, a smell so delicate and delicious I worry it will break if I inhale too deeply emanates from the kitchen below. Timmy has made breakfast, not an unusual feat since he worked in the restaurant industry for years, but there is something different about this day, this morning. I descend the stairs slowly, still rubbing the sleep from my eyes. Timmy is washing dishes as our plates sit steaming on the glass table.

"This looks good," I say with a husk still in my voice.

"It is good," he says as he clunks a frying pan into the dish drainer. He shuts off the water and slides out a chair for me to sit down.

"Whole wheat toast," he explains as he points to my plate, "and an egg white omelet with fresh veggies. Six points." He smiles wide and broad, proud of his gesture. On the kitchen counter sits my Points book, held open by a drinking glass.

My heart collapses in on itself under the weight of my gratitude. That breakfast is the best god damned breakfast I have ever had in my life. As I eat, I cannot help but allow two or three small tears to drip down my cheeks. In that moment, the contrast between my lunch with Jack and my breakfast with Timmy is stark and clear. This is where I belong, right here, with this man who has already proven in our short time together, that there is no universe big enough to keep us apart.

The next night, as I walk through the doorway into Pantsuit Pam's orbit with my head draped in shame and ten plus pounds stuck to my ass, she smiles and continues on as if I never left. Her eyes tell me that I am safe and loved.

"Welcome back," Sherri with an i whispers.

"Thanks. It's good to be home," I say.

eight months later

Chapter Forty-Two

The slide of the metal weight is one I know well. Left, lower, left, lower. A thin finger pushing, the metallic squeal, the final bounce, the balance. It's a pulse that has been present in my body for almost two years now. Only today, the scale is moving to the right. It feels unnatural. Like I'm living in a dream where things have reversed themselves.

"You're up ten pounds, Amye," a soft voice whispers.

For the first time in my life I am not panicked. Timmy has brought love and acceptance into my life in a way I have never known it. The middle of me is calm and still. I step down from the scale and am led into a dark room with a bed and a monitor.

"How many weeks are you?" a cute little old man named Ned stands between my spread legs with a plastic wand in his hands.

"I'm not sure. That's why I'm here," My head is a balloon floating over my body. I have been pregnant for two days now. At least, that's how long I have known. I had been sick to my stomach for weeks, but attributed the nausea to the new birth control pill I was taking. Then, at Georgia's suggestion, *just to rule it out*, I peed on a stick and magic happened. A second pink line pushed itself through, breaking the membrane of the sterile white screen.

Even Ned, with his gigantic wand shoved inside of me, cannot ground me in this moment. I cannot stop smiling, laughing, crying, dreaming, thanking Timmy for giving me everything I've ever wanted.

"Uh-oh, wait a second," Ned mutters and fiddles with the settings on the monitor. The images of white swirl around like a cloud pattern on a satellite view of earth.

"What's the matter?" My whole body tightens. *I knew it. This isn't real. There is no baby. It's all been a horrible mistake.*

Ned pushes the wand deeper inside of me, and suddenly a hole of blackness opens on the screen to my right. There in the center lies the most beautiful thing I have ever seen in my life. My baby. Our baby.

"Ahh, there we go," Ned says.

"But, what's that?" I ask pointing to the second white dot.

"Amye, my dear, you're having twins."

That night, as I pull the black and white picture from my purse and lay it on Timmy's lap, his eyes widen. We have just settled into our new place, a house we are renting together on Scranton's south side. The apartment in Wilkes-Barre had become too small and too scary. Two months earlier, there was a double homicide across the street. That was the end of it. We found a place that was halfway between our jobs, a small two-bedroom house in a not-so-much-better neighborhood.

I had reservations about living with someone again, especially in a new place. I had come to love that little loft, and I had grown and learned so much there. I consulted and agonized over the decision for weeks, but in the end, I just had to follow my heart. The day I handed back the keys to Faye, our building manager, I felt a surge of excitement in my body. I was starting a life with the man I love. A man who is strong, independent, honest, and hardworking. And best of all, madly in love with me.

"Are you okay?" I ask as Timmy holds the thin ultrasound photograph in his hands. He says nothing and sinks back into the tan cushion of the couch. It's dark outside, the warm June air is winding in and out of the windows behind us. We were just getting used to the surprise of a pregnancy, and now this. Twins. Since Timmy is a twin, we had joked about this occurring, but after researching the fact that fraternal twins are only carried on the mother's side, and there are no twins anywhere in my family, we thought we were safe.

"Amye," he says and lowers the picture back onto his lap. "Maybe we should get married."

Married? Was he crazy? Those were the last words I expected to hear cross his lips. Timmy and I had talked a little about marriage in the last few months, especially in the past week. We both agreed, I thought, that marriage ruins everything. I had tried it already, and I vowed I would never do it again. And now, one little glimpse of a sonogram picture and he's ready to throw away all of our convictions?

"What do you think?" he presses when I don't answer.

"I…I thought we agreed that we would never…"

"Amye," he turns to me, holds my small sweaty hands in his, "I love you. We're going to be a family."

"I know but that doesn't mean …" I can't even talk, my tongue is thick and strange in my mouth.

Timmy strokes my hair with one hand, and his hazel eyes stare right through me. "What do you say? Will you marry me?" In that moment, I can almost see our whole future together. Next month, we will stand in front of a Magistrate with only our parents, Jennie, and Ollie at our sides. I will suffer from horrible carpal tunnel during my pregnancy, and will gladly trade my guitar playing for my growing belly. In another six months, I will quit my job and we will welcome our daughters, Samantha and Penelope, into the world. They will be exactly ten months and three days younger than Georgia's new daughter. The exact same age difference between Georgia and me.

Then, Timmy and I will buy my grandmother's house, the home she loved. The home where my father was raised. In her home, we will live peacefully and happily as a family. Timmy will work ten, twelve hour days as a carpenter and come home so exhausted he can barely keep his eyes open. Yet, he will stay with our baby girls as I attend an MFA program and pursue my writing, just like I promised Sergio and Heather I would.

But I can't see any of that now from our couch in the dense summer night. I can only see a promise; a glimmer of what's to come. When I look at him, a warmth comes over me. A feeling of recognition. Like this is the home I have been searching for all along.

"Yes," I whisper, "I will marry you."

And somehow I know that now is the time for hope.

Interview with Amye Archer

Being overweight is a very sensitive topic. Did you approach this project with any qualms?

I did. I felt a strange responsibility to my sisters-in-weight to "get it right." One thing I had to keep in mind is that body image is relative. A woman's relationship with her body is a private and very personal space. I didn't want to violate that space, or make light of it in any way. I tried my best to stay respectful, while still writing as truthfully as I could.

What parts of this book were most painful to write?

There are parts of this book that still make me cringe. I read it and I find myself yelling at that stupid girl in the backseat of someone's car. But I think the most painful stuff to write had to do with my food addiction. I like to think that it was painful because I've conquered that demon, but I don't think you ever really do. I'm sober right now, but my sobriety is a daily struggle, and some days it is harder than others to stay away from my drug of choice. Many people who are in my life right now don't know this side of me, and it's terrifying to put myself out there in this way. But I had to be honest, I had to try my best to capture the true way in which food addicts live: binary. We are either sober or not sober, in control or not in control. There is seldom a middle ground.

What did you learn about yourself while you were writing this book?

I spent many years feeling responsible for someone else. For a very long time my life was not my own. I felt that my ex-husband's mental health depended on me in some way, when in reality, I was making it worse. The single biggest lesson I learned while writing *Fat Girl, Skinny* is that I will never give my life over to anyone else, ever again.

I also feel like writing this book was therapy for me. I started writing it in 2009, and finished four years and seven major revisions later.

Throughout that time, I discovered things about my marriage that helped me come to terms with what had happened. There was a lot of forgiving that had to happen, yes I forgave him, but more importantly, I had to forgive myself.

What was it like writing about real people? Did you worry about how they would react?

I did. I still worry. As writers, we joke about the fact that if you hurt us, burn us, or even love us, you could show up in a book someday. And while that might sound funny, it's really not. The people in this book, through no fault of their own, were involved in some capacity with a memoir writer. They just didn't know it yet. I took great lengths to protect some of them. I changed names, changed some minor details about their lives, and deliberately omitted some things that I thought wouldn't affect the story. It's a tough decision, to write memoir. I could have called this fiction and made my life a lot easier, but I thought it was important to tell my truth about this topic. So many women struggle with food addiction, weight, and low self-esteem. I hope that this book makes them feel-less alone in that world. To do that, it had to be real.

Tell us about Pantsuit Pam. How did she influence your weight loss journey?

Pantsuit Pam is a composite of official and "unofficial" Weight Watchers leaders I've encountered during my time in the program. I wanted to take the best pieces of advice I had received and share them with the reader without having to introduce nine other minor characters. The physical appearance of Pantsuit Pam and her mannerisms are based on one specific person, but the wisdom she imparts comes from several sources. So I will say this: while Pantsuit Pam influenced me greatly, it was the Weight Watchers program in general that led to a healthier, slimmer me.

Why the title Fat Girl, Skinny?

This book never had another title, which is more that I can say for everything else I've written. I wanted something that would symbolize what I believe is the core message in the book, that is, fat is a state of mind; it's something internal that you must adjust, not simply an external state of being that can be "fixed." So I wanted to essentially tell the story of a skinny fat girl, hence, I needed the comma. This is the story of a fat girl, skinny.

What do you hope to leave others with?

I hope that my readers will be left with a sense of hope and the realization that you must create a support network for yourself if you hope to get well.

We have so many systems of support in place for addicts of every variety—yet food addicts are still largely marginalized in society. Underneath the story of weight loss and divorce, *Fat Girl, Skinny* is the story of how I created a world of my own within myself. I took up hobbies, made new friends, and tried things that took me out of my comfort zone. But, most importantly, I was patient. I gave myself the time I needed to heal. The day my husband left me, my sister Jennie said to me "In a year, you won't recognize your life." I will never forget that sentence. Nothing heals the wounds of heartbreak faster than time.

Printed in Great Britain
by Amazon